DREAMING
THE DAWN

Dreaming the Dawn

E. K. CALDWELL

CONVERSATIONS
WITH NATIVE
ARTISTS AND
ACTIVISTS

Introduction by Elizabeth Woody

University of Nebraska
Lincoln and London

Acknowledgments for
the use of previously
published material
appear on page vii

Library of Congress
Cataloging-in-
Publication Data
Caldwell, E. K., 1954–
Dreaming the dawn :
conversations with
native artists and
activists / E. K.
Caldwell; introduction
by Elizabeth Woody.
p.   cm. – (American
Indian lives)
ISBN 0-8032-1500-2
(cl. : alk. paper)
1. Indian artists –
North America –
Interviews. 2. Indian
activists – North
America – Interviews.
I. Title   II. Series.
E98.A7C15   1999
970.004'97–dc21
98-51490   CIP

CONTENTS

All photos © Vicki
Grayland, except
Buffy Sainte-Marie,
© David Gahr, and
Litefoot, courtesy
James Caldwell.

PREFACE

The interviews included here reflect the thoughts and feelings of real native people. There has been and continues to be a romanticization or maligning of who and what the indigenous people of this continent represent. This book doesn't use the "dog and pony show" concept of keeping people's attention with tricks of entertainment and illusions of pseudospirituality. The people in this book are real people, living real lives and dealing with the ongoing struggle of being indigenous people in a land that has been overrun with a dominant values system that affects indigenous people as well as whites. The people represented here have come to terms with certain things within themselves, and their words have brought their own kind of understanding to many who have previously read these interviews when they appeared between 1993 and 1997 in *News from Indian Country: The Nation's Native Journal*, published in Hayward, Wisconsin. Versions of many of these interviews also were published during the same time period in *Inkfish Magazine* on the Oregon coast.

I would like to thank all those represented in these pages for taking the time to talk with me and for trusting that their words would be presented as accurately as possible. It has been an honor to do this work.

E. K. Caldwell
June 1997

INTRODUCTION

ELIZABETH WOODY

I met Kim in the winter of 1991 at a four-star resort called Salishan
Lodge. A mutual friend, Yurok artist and blues musician Rick Bartow,
kept after me to meet Kim. He said, "She's a fine writer, just starting
out, and a real good person, to boot." Well, Kim had been writing for
some time, but she was a little shy about it. Through the years, she and I
became close friends. We all encouraged her to apply for the fellowship
to attend the first Returning the Gift, a conference for native storytellers and writers of North America held in Norman, Oklahoma, in
1992. I wrote a letter of support for her. We even shared a room there
and subsequently traveled to other places together, like the Rocky
Mountain Book Festival and the southwest Wordcraft Circle conference in Chinle, Arizona. Kim was community oriented and very supportive of young women writers. She often paid her own way to conferences and gave out gifts in generous quantities. She had several
apprentice writers and an ever widening circle of accomplished writers
she communicated with on a regular basis, myself included. She often
would call on me to send out some prayers for someone or to chat about
the scene.

   She was an honest person, painfully so. Kim never let anyone slip
into self-pity or pull the wool over the eyes of another. She could tell me
a story in just the right words, making my spine tingle with the electric-
ity of truth. Very few have struck that kind of nerve in me, and for that
quality I miss her dearly. We talked about some very serious business,
like the extinction of salmon, the question of how kids are going to live
in the growing mess of human indulgence and waste, and why being a
modern Indian woman is hard work.

   Kim made me laugh and tolerated my eccentricities. Like the time
she and I drove for six straight hours after the Chinle conference, and

then I insisted we drive another fifty miles round trip to get my dog, Uppittee. We found Uppittee sleeping on the couch at Gloria Bird's house, with the TV on and the door locked. I could see my dog from the living room window, and Gloria was nowhere in sight. When I returned to the car, Kim said to me, "Dang! It must be love!! We drove an extra fifty miles to look at her sleeping." I felt so bad. Kim was very exhausted, and maybe in pain from fibromyalgia.

Earlier at Kim's beautiful house at the beach, Uppittee was walking on a ledge that went around her house. If this wasn't bad enough, the ledge was sixty-some feet above the crashing waves of the Pacific Ocean. My dog stood there with the wind in her ears, peeking at Kim and I talking in the dining room, and I freaked! Kim said, "Don't worry, just call her in like you always do." She knew I loved my pooch big. At Kim's funeral, a little girl came up to me and said, "Hey, are you the lady with the dog laying on the couch watching TV, and you had to drive all that way to see her?"

There were a few things we had in common besides our friends. We both loved our grandmothers, survived house fires, and had a psychic ability—a state of awareness she knew well, but one that I was only beginning to recognize. Feelings, trust, separating imagination from true vision, she was good at that.

We both were big, in laughter, voice, and body. She, I imagine, hadn't felt these qualities to be unendurable. I read her poem "When Big Women Get the Blues" for her family and friends at the funeral as we were saying good-bye. Some said it was a "cute" poem. I am intensely passionate, and being a big Indian woman, I sometimes scare people, especially the slender women who suffer and deprive themselves to meet an unnatural standard. Somewhere, American women's form changed into commodity. Kim was not a commodity, but another passionate original.

Kim belted out the blues and did R&B, rock, and jazz vocals. This was something I didn't know until after her death. She also played acoustic guitar and became well known for her beautiful voice and lyrical knack. She played in a women's trio called Queen Bee and the Drones. She had the soul for singing and for expression that comes from the center of one's being.

She started out her seventeen-year career as a counselor with the Abraxus Foundation in Pennsylvania. Eventually Kim worked with inmates at the Correctional Treatment Program for the state of Oregon. Kim's soul was one filtered through the fire of firsthand experience with addiction and subsequent incarceration and through personal loss, losing a dear friend in a brutal murder right after graduating from the Abraxus program herself. On her way to her new job in Oregon, she and James "Snail" Caldwell rekindled their relationship. They married a few years later.

Snail told me about Kim's background and her life. Some details Kim didn't share, but I could intuit. She was the eldest of four children. Kim survived two house fires when she was a girl. I had survived only one, myself. Her father, Dave Conner, worked as a boilermaker, constructing coal furnaces and nuclear power plants around Pennsylvania. This was hard work, and deaths were common. Still, it beat working in the woods and carrying logs on your back, as Dave did before. Snail explained to me that in order to understand this area, southwestern Pennsylvania, you had to understand that people were exposed to immigrant cultures on an ongoing basis. You grew up street smart and tough. Kim's folks were Tsalagi—German on her mom's side and Shawnee-Irish on her dad's. Kim's maternal great-grandmother, Minnie, taught her from their Native American heritage, Tsalagi. She insisted that Shirly, Kim's mother, have the middle name of Iona, Bear, and that Kim's middle name be Kiona, Little Bear. Kim's middle name was Kimberly, but her true name was Kiona.

When Kim was eleven, she was a little overweight. In the 1960s amphetamines were not considered dangerous for weight loss. One drug led to another, but in spite of these dark times, Kim sang in a choir at a Baptist church. Most of her friends as a teenager were African American. She was offered a scholarship to the Carnegie-Mellon University in music, but enticed by the excellent theatrical program at Clarion State College, she opted instead to attend it as a journalism major. A love of music came from her family's involvement with Sunday Bluegrass at maternal grandmother Estelle's. Her maternal grandfather, also important to Kim, was a coal miner and died of the black lung.

Another thing that Kim and I had in common and that came up in our lives but that may not have been an issue even ten or fifty years ago is blood quantum. Kim was not enrolled. Her folks weren't into it. Even if I marry, my spouse would have to be a full blood to have kids eligible for enrollment in any one of my tribal ancestries. Kim took people at face value. She wasn't judgmental, as long as you did what you said you would do and kept your word. She knew what being an "Indian" was about. I never knew her people, her family, but I knew that her associates and her colleagues were spiritual people. Kim was a spiritual person, too. This spiritual recognition of her lineage came from the Creator, not from the government. At her funeral, eagles came and circled the house; at the funeral home, an eagle came to help us. Kim and Snail were setting up the creek near their house as a rehabilitated fish habitat and hatchery. The Salmon Conservation Corps kids, from the Columbia River Basin tribes, helped. Later, two of them approached me after a lecture, telling me Kim made them feel "real special," like they were "really making a difference" and that she "believed in them." That she did; she made us all feel like we were very special, really doing something to make a difference.

What we have of her intelligence and ability to make connections in many fields of human activity are in these interviews and a manuscript of poetry. Kim decided to devote herself full time to writing in 1992. For that we must thank her husband, Snail, who supported this endeavor. She had a great organizational ability, sifting through enormous amounts of information to find the right questions. Once, when she mailed a list of questions for an interview to Vine Deloria, he wrote back, "I'd have to write a whole other book to answer all this." She was perceptive and thorough. She often became pressured in the last few years of her writing life, with her energy low and like myself suffering from chronic illness, and she developed "brain fog." That's what makes these interviews interesting—her thoroughness and attention to detail. She was a lifelong learner and teacher. The folks she interviewed were friends, or friends of friends. Her circle was perhaps a limited one, because they were all Indian, but one that represents communities stretched out in activity, making sure something better happens for the kids and for the land. Kim was like that; she was a community builder. I hope we learn from her and can all share our lives as well, like this.

JOHN TRUDELL

John Trudell has been labeled and categorized for the past twenty years by the U.S. government, the American Indian Movement (AIM), the entertainment industry, the listening public, the media, and, not least of all, himself. He has been called radical, militant, political activist, visionary, subversive, poet, writer, and many other labels. He spoke about the dangers of the labels given to us by ourselves and others when he addressed a group of new, young writers that gathered for the Wordcraft Circle Native Writers Regional Workshop in Newport, Oregon, in late October 1993. He encouraged them to express their true voices and to recognize the difference between the persona of "the writer" and the many facets of who they really are—as one of the People.

"As we take on these labels, we must remember that they describe what we do, not who we are. We are the People—we are human beings—that's who we are. We have to accept all the parts of us as being part of a whole. When I called myself a 'political activist' and started saying that's *who I was,* then that's all I saw. I didn't see a lot of important things, and I missed a lot of things. I was locked in there and looked at only a part of me as being the total. It's the same with the label 'writer' or any other label. It limits us if we confuse what we do with who we are. At the basic core of reality, we're human beings. If we don't forget that, it will help make our way a little better. We are the People. Our ancestors and the ancient ones were the People. And I am just one of the People, doing the best I can with the best I've got." The writers attending the workshop were responsive to Trudell's words and also to the attention he gave to them individually by making himself accessible for conversation.

At the Nye Beach Hotel on October 23, 1993, we had an opportunity to talk about his benefit performance for the Wordcraft workshop with his performing ensemble, Tribal Voice (Trudell, Quiltman, and Tewahnee), and about his perceptions regarding the voices of the new, young writers and the issues in the community that affect these voices.

E. K. CALDWELL: People responded really well to hearing Tribal Voice again after such a long time. How did it feel being Tribal Voice after being accustomed to being with the band?

JOHN TRUDELL: Yeah, it's been a long time since Quilt and I did any Tribal Voice. Actually, it felt pretty good. I've been thinking about maybe doing more.

C: Are you thinking about doing any new tapes of Tribal Voice?

T: That's interesting that you should bring that up because I was just talking to Quilt about [how] maybe we should make a new Tribal Voice tape. I would really be interested in doing that.

C: In coming to this gathering with new writers, and in doing the Peace with Earth tour that benefited Oregon Native Youth Council and in other communities on that tour that are working with youth in the community—well, is this a beginning in this phase of your evolution? Are you going to other parts of the country and talking with writers and students and young people?

T: I'm not really looking at any of it as a starting place. I'm glad that young people are relating to my work, and it's good if there's any positive influences that this has upon them. I'm glad the young people are amongst the people that I'm working with because I've been wandering around for many years now doing things. And this is really the first time I'm seeing the results of people in the community working with young people and therefore giving me an opportunity to do it. The thing that I try to be careful of is that, you know, I'm just me. And I'm liable to do anything at any given time. So I don't look that I'm a "role model," or that I'm someone to be pointed out as being the better person. I'm just another person. Whatever good or coherency I have to contribute, if people can be influenced or communicated to by that, then I'm glad. But it's very important to me that the community allows me to just be a person and not to set these unreal standards on me [*laughs*] that even the community can't live by. I'm doing the best I can with the best I got. But if I allow people to say, "Well, he's the role model" or he's something he's not, then these are the people in the end who will attack me when I can't fulfill their expectations.

c: One of my nine-year-old nieces asked her mom about why so many of your songs are about women and how they feel about things. I think that's an interesting observation coming from a nine-year-old girl, and would like to ask your response to that.

t: It is interesting that one so young would notice that. Well, I don't know. One thing I would like to say is that women have been much better to me than I have been to them. And maybe in some way, it's like an apology. It's just that at some point it came into my mind to *try*, because that's the best thing that I can do because I am a male, but to try to express how women feel. And either I would be able to do it or I wouldn't be able to do it. So any ability I have to do it, I have no explanation for. I do know the basic reality that the women are done wrong and have been done wrong by more than the males—by a mind-set, by a perception of life and that we're all trapped in it. And maybe, in some abstract way, it's a way of trying to make penance. [*Laughs*] But I don't know. It may be that I've worn too many black hats, and like I have to say it now, because I've been wearing the black hat too long. I'm a good person, but I don't always do good things, whether it's in relationship to women or men or whatever it is. It depends on what kind of attitude I have or [*laughs*] who's taken control of my mind for the day or the moment. And I'm really not all that good at it—about women I mean. [*Laughing*] I know that I live by myself, whatever it is, [*still laughing*] so I have to keep that reality in mind.

c: How do you feel about other poets or musicians using the kind of format that is associated primarily with your work?

t: Yeah, I have no problem with it. When I started to do this, they were looking at the high-tech "sound" as being innovative. Well, I think I saw this point where I thought, "A new human energy is what it's going to take to change this." So, that's where I decided to enter into it with what we call the poetry, the spoken word. My intention has always been to get as far as I can with it, and maybe others will go after it, too. I'm not threatened by it. I'm glad for it. Anytime it means I'm not out there by myself, [*laughs*] well, then that's a good thing, right?

C: Some of the younger writers who are poets equate you with "rock 'n' roll star" status and assume they can make a lot of money putting their work out there. Some folks seem to be getting the impression that you are becoming very affluent.

T: [*Laughing*] Well, it is definitely a mistaken impression. Don't expect poetry to make you rich in dollars. Don't write poetry because you think you're going to make money out of it. I would say about the money part of it is that, if they write what they feel and they make the writing about that, then money may come in various forms and ways for different ones of them because that's the kind of world we deal with. I have reasons to do this other than the money I'm going to make. If my reasons for doing this are fulfilled and I'm effective, then there will probably be money. But money would be a result—it's not the goal. Right now, [*laughing*] it's not a result, either.

C: Two of your daughters have been performing with you with the band and with Tribal Voice. How are you feeling about working with them?

T: On that *Children of Earth* tape, my daughter, Star, was about six, and she had some children's tape she had gotten, *Snow White* or something. I was listening to that, and I thought we need to have some children's tapes that talk about reality, and use the children's voices to say it. So I set out to write some lyrics to that effect. I have three daughters, so I picked which ones would read each part. I want them to understand the process without having too much placed on them and becoming overwhelmed by it. That way all they have to do is relax and go in there and do it the best that they can. And I think that they did a really good job considering our working realities. When we got ready to go out and perform it, I was very pleased with how they handled that. It's not like they don't get nervous, because that's natural on stage at first. But when they're on stage and performing, it's like, well, if you forget a line, don't worry about it. Another thing that's coming out of this [is] that they are learning how to deal with very public situations. So, I think that it's good for them and healthy for them.

C: Are they writing?

T: [*Smiling*] Yeah, they're starting to—I want them to write some of their own lyrics. We have maybe two or three things that they've written that will really work. The way I'm approaching it is that they write, and after enough time passes, we'll pick what can be used. I figure the next album we make with the girls, they will have some of their own writing on it.

C: Would you talk more about encouraging writers to write the truth of their experience?

T: As writers, we need to say the truth about how we feel. I don't mean express or say things we think other people want to hear. We should express the truth of how we feel. I think that a part of that is we need to look at or analyze the words we use. Especially as writers. How we use the words has a lot to do with it because every word has some kind of a concept that goes with it. Sometimes we use words where the concept doesn't fit what we're really trying to say. Knowing what we're saying ourselves is what makes the communication. That's what going to connect with other people. For me, I just started writing these things down, and I think that any value people have found in my writing has been around that feelings got communicated. It was more than just making sense. To me, it's just to write what I feel and to look at these words that I'm using. I don't try to get people to agree or disagree with me. If I write something and put it out there, and people say, "Well, you're really nuts, and I don't agree with that"—then that's their problem, not mine. If people say "Well, we really like this, and we really relate to this," then there is no problem. But, either way, I'm still going to write what I feel.

c: And what would you suggest to the younger, newer writers in terms of maintaining their sense of the truth?

t: Be as real as you can be. Do the best that you can with the best that you have. And that's all we can do. But you see, it's enough. When I say that's all we can do, I don't mean it in a context that it's minimal. I mean that it is enough because we all have that ability. And if we would all do that, I mean in the grand scheme of things, it's enough. Question our own truths. We should always question our own truths, too.

c: In terms of our relationship in the world, you talked about the influence of the patriarchal religions imposed on us and how this disconnects people from the earth as mother. Do you think that because people, particularly in America, don't have ties to their own ancestral land base that this contributes to the acquisition and domination of the land base of others? Do you think they're "motherless" because they don't have connection to the land of their ancestors?

t: No, I think it's just because they don't have connection to the land anywhere. Maybe you're right that when you get way down into the roots and the causes of things that they don't have a relationship to their own ancestral land and that contributes to why these problems exist. But I think that, at this time, it's not having a connection to the earth. Anywhere. I have seen people from the tribes, "Indians," that don't have that connection. Somehow it got taken from them. They may have certain blood degrees, but they don't have the connection. So it has to do with being separated from our relationship to the earth entirely.

c: You mention about "regardless of their blood degrees." There seems to be an acceleration lately in the controversy about who has the Certified Degree of Indian Blood [CDIB] cards and who are the "real Indians." What do you think about all that going on?

t: About the cards and stuff, right—well, the Jews didn't go running around Europe quarreling with one another because they didn't have a number tattooed on their arm. You know, reality. Besides, none of us are "Indians" so it's a meaningless quarrel about who's the "most Indian" or who's the "best Indian." We're the People—we come from the tribes, and that's who the ancient ones were and who the ancestors were—the People.

c: Do you think that this quarrel going on is just a continuation of the original genocide plan?

T: Yes, it is. It's just a continuation of divide and conquer, right? I look at it as a sign, a symptom. When people will spend all their time to quarrel about these things, then I look at it as a fear, that people are afraid to deal with what the real problem is. It's a classic system among the oppressed to take it out on each other, among yourselves, while your oppressor continues to have his way with you. And I think that to some degree, that applies here. And then there are those people who try to identify and take what little economic services that are to be provided to the tribal people. There are people there who are saying they are from the tribes or they are "Indian" because they think they can get a free ride. All these things are mixed in there, but I think the community knows who the People are and who they aren't. Because I know to me, as one person, I don't want to deal with any Nazis—and I don't care what color they are or what their cultural affiliation is, but if they carry that Nazi trip, then they don't get it. Another thing that I find interesting about it is that there are many, many mixed-blood people now, right? I mean, I'm a mixed blood, and I accept who I am, and I have a role to play in this world and in this society, and my identity is my identity, and I don't want to fight with my own people. I don't have time to quarrel with them. And I see them quarrel amongst themselves about who's the "real Indian" and who isn't, and to me that's a meaningless quarrel.

c: What do you think this quarrel does to our young people?

T: It confuses them. Because what it's saying to the young people, especially the mixed-blood young people, is, "You have no validity." It says to them, "You're not real." It's a form of attacking our young, based upon the prejudices and the bitternesses of an older generation. Sometimes people don't really understand what they're doing. And I think that it's time to sort a lot of this out in the sense of, "Well, look, things need to be made better for the People, and that's what we should be looking at," right? To make things better for the People, not to create new dictators who say, "Hey, to be an 'Indian,' you've got to be like this—to be a traditionalist, you have to be like this." The practical reality of this quarrel is there are more tribal people that are unrecognized by the federal government than are recognized. That's a deliberate policy. I know "Indians" who live in cities because they were placed there a generation ago through relocation and things, and it doesn't make these people any less People—it's just that they were raised somewhere else. But the government's not going to recognize them as "Indians" because they're not on the tribal rolls somewhere. And it's a form of termination. Controlling our identity.

c: When you spoke to the writers, you spoke about how we can limit our identity with labels, whether that's "writer" or "political activist" or whatever. Do you think that CDIB cards can do that, too?

t: Yes, the whole concept does. Because then you can't be a total person, you can only be a part of a person, and that's the part that fits the image of the things you say you are.

c: [Some of the] things you talked about were some of the realities of AIM and the quarrels about who the leaders were and quarrels that have been carried over into these times. A lot of people have a tendency to romanticize those struggles, especially the media. It seems that in coverage about you, people have a tendency to concentrate only on the past. Like your life stopped in 1979. How do you feel about that?

t: In relationship to me and when it's happening to me, I think that these are people who don't want to face the realities of now. A lot of times people will write an article about me, and they don't have a clue what they're doing. In their quest to be "objective," they become very nondescript, or in wanting to be what they call "creative," they want to lay this "angry Indian" thing on me. They take up what they think is a unique thing, but it's really just a repetitious, redundant story that's been done in a lot of places. They try to lock me into all that angry, restless, militant this and that and my lifestyle to that point. To me it's a lack of creativity, and if one is truly a journalist, then it's an irresponsibility as a journalist. Basically, to me, it's really a sign of laziness.

c: In terms of the work you are doing now—how would you put that into words for those PR packets that go out of the office in California?

t: I'm not sure how to do that. [*Laughing*] Basically, I'm really uncooperative with them. That whole idea of bios and publicity and things, well, I would say as little as possible. My bio would be my name and my age. [*Laughing*] Like this name survived this long, and that's the history. I don't want to praise myself, [*laughing*] and I sure don't want to condemn myself, or expose myself, and it's a fine line. So, I do have to take responsibility for that, too, in terms of what the PR people put out there.

c: Who do you read?

t: Nobody.

c: Nobody at all?

t: Once in a while I may find something that I can really get into reading, but it takes a certain focus for me to sit down and read. [*Laughs*] It seems like my attention span just gets shorter and shorter. If [it] isn't short, I don't really read it anymore. I used to do a lot of reading when I was in college. I read a lot of Black Hawk and Handsome Lake, and the things that they said made sense to me and were true to me. At that time I read many things. *The Autobiography of Malcolm X* had a profound and tremendous influence on me. Malcolm X influenced me about honesty in a way that no one else has because he was not afraid to say who he was. And I remember reading that book and thinking, "I wish I could do that—to just say it and not try to cover it up—and if you don't want it known, then don't say it. And not be afraid to say the truth." And that had a tremendous amount of influence on me—that one particular book. Through the course of the

70s I read a lot of what we would call political publications. My initial choice, I guess I would say, is to read the things that have a different view of what's going on than what we're being told in the newspapers and on the television.

C: In terms of music, who has influenced you there, especially since *AKA Graffiti Man* and the new release *Johnny Damas and Me* are contemporary in their musical aspects?

T: I like a lot of kinds of music. My real interest is in what the singers are saying. I listened to Buffy Sainte-Marie and Bob Dylan and John Lennon and Kris Kristofferson and John Prine. People that were storytellers—people that said things that were real. At some point in their careers, they made this kind of music. These things had a tremendous influence on me because that's where I first picked up on some realities. People of our generation came of age in a time when the music was about the people, and you had songs like "Universal Soldier" and people like Buffalo Springfield singing "For What It's Worth." These lyrics were addressing certain realities. The young people were out there, and we were active, and we were making ourselves visible. This is the advantage that we had, right? At that point in America, the insiders who controlled the business side of it said, "This music is too dangerous, so it's got to be changed," and then they led it into acid rock and heavy metal and disco and things that would take it away from that lyrical content. I would suggest that people listen to all kinds of music, especially if you want to put your words to music, because the music has its own feel, too. Also, listen to the writers—to the ones who really say things. For the young people today, I don't know how they would relate to John Lennon's coherence. But I think it's worth listening to, because an album that had the equivalent effect on me to *The Autobiography of Malcolm X* was an album that John Lennon made with the Plastic Ono Band after the breakup of the Beatles. And his song "Working Class Hero," that really turned my head around—it really did something—that one particular song. What I admired about him was when he got in there and [*big smile*] he screamed and he yelled and he didn't hold any of it back, and I thought, now here's a level of honesty I can relate to—I mean, I don't have it, but I can relate to it—the same way I could relate to what Malcolm X was saying. It reflected the truth to me.

C: Do you think rap music accurately reflects the truth of the urban youth and their experience?

T: No, I don't think it reflects their reality—I think it's programming their reality. I think it started out reflecting a reality, and they were saying what they had to say. Now the suits have stepped in, the insiders in the suits, and now they say, "You've all got to sound like this and be like this." So it's a way of trapping it and limiting it within that context. There are more realities going on in the communities of young people than what the rappers sing about. But because they want to "make it," now they have to stay within the confines of the realities that have been defined for them. And that programs them in a way that's not good for anybody.

C: The concluding thing that I'd like to ask you to speak to is, how does it feel to hear all these young writers' words? Your generosity in coming to participate in Wordcraft Circle brought out a full house of people to hear Tribal Voice, and that resulted in many student writers being heard by those people. How's that feel?

T: It makes me feel good. Really good, actually. Some people misunderstand, you know, what it's all about for me. In many ways, this is what it's really all about. It's not about money. And it's not about fame. It's about being a part of a larger group. When I first started writing poetry, it wasn't something that "men" did, especially coming out of the militants—it just wasn't. It isn't that people raised hell with me or anything, but there was a certain awkwardness about it in certain places in the community. It's good to see that whole notion has been set aside. Let's take it beyond writing poetry or writing—it's about expressing how we feel, and I truly feel there has not been enough of that going on in our generation. We've been expressing our anger, but we haven't been expressing how we feel. Basically when life re-

volves around just venting the anger, then that's about emotional reaction. I'm glad that I can be a part of where people are saying what
they feel now, and not just emotionally reacting. It takes me back to
the very beginning when I first entered the activism—it was about us
expressing how we feel. But it became something else. And then we
could no longer express what we felt. We had organizations and political thought and political structure and the realms of that. It's like
we've come back now to where we started, but this time it's with a
younger group of people, a more open group of people. And that, to
me, is a good feeling for our future.

ELIZABETH WOODY

The ancestry of her birth (Warm Springs and Wasco/Navajo, both Oregon tribes) has gifted Elizabeth Woody with a special voice—a voice that is strongly shaped by the land and the prayers it raises in the hearts of indigenous people, a voice that knows the contemporary world and understands that survival of those who inhabit the land depends on the principles of ancient tradition.

Woody's work has been widely anthologized and published nationally and internationally. Her first collection of poetry, *Hand into Stone*, won the 1990 American Book Award. Well-known author Barry Lopez commented, "revealing and self assured, her images are remarkable. . . . this is a wonderful voice." Native poet Gail Tremblay best summarized Woody's contribution with eloquent simplicity, "Earth is richer for this voice."

Two newer volumes of work, *Luminaries of the Humble* (University of Arizona Press, Sun Tracks Series) and *Seven Hands, Seven Hearts* (Eighth Mountain Press) were released within months of one another in the autumn of 1994. This is no small accomplishment in the poetry publishing world. That same autumn she became a professor of creative writing at the Institute of American Indian Arts (IAIA), where she continues to teach. As generous with her thoughts as she is with her laughter, Elizabeth Woody represents contemporary native writing at its finest.

E. K. CALDWELL: In recent articles and essays and discussions, many native writers seem to be addressing the issue of native writers' "place" in literature. In an essay you and Gloria Bird wrote, "The Rim of the World," you talk about native writing being an "ethnic fragment." What does that mean?

ELIZABETH WOODY: When Gloria and I talked about "ethnic fragment," we were saying that American literature seems to fragment itself. The canon, brought from Europe, is a very brief part of the literary history on this continent. The literary history, the land itself, and the cultures upon it go back more than a millennium, go back to time immemorial. The literature that we draw upon as people and as writers has some attachment to the new American literature, but it also has a bigger affinity and relationship to history and traditional oral narrative and to the history of families because the nature of oral tradition is oftentimes more truthful. When we're dissociated from the natural literature common to us, we begin to lose a sense of ourselves. Then we are willing the accept the "ethnic fragment" position.

C: Craig Lesley was quoted as saying that he sees the 90s as being a "literary renaissance" for native writers. What kind of voice do you think we bring to contemporary literature?

EW. Well, I think basically we have an honest voice. I hear a lot of discussions about how so and so is buying into the stereotypes or the "media Indian" or creating literature that suits the white mainstream culture, and there may be some of that, but for the most part the writers who are coming into being now have integrity.

The literature I am interested in is powerful literature by authors like Leslie Marmon Silko. In *Almanac of the Dead*, where she talks almost prophetically about our salvation and revolution coming from the South, from Latin America, which is predominantly Native American. She says that we oftentimes will feel on the verge of collapse, in terms of the economy. This is because the United States operates without integrity. Throughout history, any direct involvement with Indian people has been without integrity and scruples. This experience can teach [non-native] people they are not far from being dispossessed and impoverished. That the same kind of mind-set will exploit anything or anybody.

I read a quote from traditional Mohawk chief Tom Porter, and he said, "The Mohawk people have a prophecy that one day our children will speak to the world, and I'm realizing now that this is the time our children are going to be speaking, and our children are the writers." That may sound ambiguous, but if you are familiar with the Iroquois Confederacy and the Tree of Peace and the Great Laws of Peace, they signify that what we have to offer humanity and the world are societies based on peace, common wealth, common good, and consensual and participatory kinds of government. Everybody is given respect for what they can contribute, so no one feels power- less—you feel like you've given something, done something, and whatever you've given has been valued.

c: Many people believe that native writing, regardless of the subject matter, is inherently political because of our historical and current relationship to the system. Do you think that's true?

w: We're born into a political status, and I don't think people are aware of the politics of their existence. Going back to the Iroquois, they speak of spirituality being the highest form of political conscious- ness. And it's when people exercise their religious freedom that they are the most oppressed. To believe in something different from Western Christianity or Judaism, or even Islam, is dangerous. I think that the spiritual and political state that you're in when you're a spiritual being is maybe threatening. It's also freeing.

If you're a free being, you're going to be very conscious of regard. You're going to be very conscious of people going in and cutting down trees. All those things will make you an active person. If you're a spiritually full person, then you will do something to stop or to pro- tect or to guide or to speak or to shape what's happening in the world around you. And the essence of being writers, of being people who pray—because prayer is part of literature—by being practitioners of word power, we affect the world.

c: That carries a lot of responsibility. What are your observations about the responsibilities writers carry in terms of impacting society?

w: I don't think I can say what that is. It's different for each person. If you're not following along with your gifts that have been given to you, you get shown real quick what you're doing wrong. I remember when I first started writing, I felt so wonderful. I found something that meant a lot to me. I found a place where I could go and talk about books, about thoughts, and about history in all kinds of different contexts. But I was reckless with all of that enthusiasm, and I began to realize that I was trying to exert some kind of control or manipulate relationships with people, like, "I'm the poet. I'm the word person, listen to me. I'm smart. I'm great." And . . . well, a lot of things happened to me. I learned that it's important for me to be willing to take care of what I say, what I do, how I relate to people, how I love them, and how I let them love me. Those are relationship things, but those are the things that come with being a poet.

c: What do you think about writers, native and non-native, who are pandering to New Age mentality in their commercialization of native spirituality? It's become a highly lucrative venture in the popular culture.

w: I can't go around and tell people who's right and who's wrong, but there are always going to be people who are opportunistic—Indian, non-Indian, or whatever race or culture—that's the choice they make. I don't buy their books, and I don't recommend their books. People who need them are basically the kind of people they are going to attract. It can be real power mongering. When you abuse the gifts that are given to you and you abuse knowledge, you may think you're smart because nothing seems to be happening to you, but it may happen two generations down, or it could happen to somebody around you.

EKC.What about the impact on those doing the buying, reading, consuming?

w: [*Long pause*] That's hard to know exactly. Say you teach a person to use fire like a tool to make life easier. If they have no respect for fire, they will be consumed. I think that's probably a good analogy.

c: What are your comments on people who are presenting traditional stories as children's books?

w: People misconstrue these stories as "children's stories." Most of the damage being done is by taking stories, making them cartoonish and putting them on TV with major parts omitted. All that's left is a caricature, a very shallow story. When the stories are taken out of context, I think that can be very damaging.

In the older days, children weren't separate from the community. They heard these stories because they were in the house when stories were told. What they absorbed at that time was only limited to what their experience was. As they got older, they remembered a story, and it hit them differently, or they heard it again, and it seemed totally different. It's the same with books.

I think the problem you're really describing is the paternalistic attitude the publishing industry has towards other cultures' stories. That, "Well, it doesn't mean anything to me, so it must be a children's story," or "it must be fantasy," or "it's an exaggeration." They put it in a category for children. It's more a judgment from the people who are publishing than from the people who are reading it. I would like to see more children's stories that are geared towards Indian children. To be read to them by their parents. There are children who are living nowhere near their communities, so these stories may be the only thing they have to relate to. People are starving from a very young age for something that is authentic, something meaningful.

c: You mentioned the attitude of publishers. What kind of access do you think native writers have to publishing?

w: Probably more now than ten years ago. Then there were only a certain number of native writers who were actually known. The expectations of those reading Native American literature only thought of those people. They had, and continue to have, access to the bigger publishing houses.

The main thing a lot of people need to understand about mainstream publishing is that it's a big business. You're a commodity. It's who you know, then what you know, that will get you anywhere. How you're going to cope with that will ultimately determine whether or not you're going to be successful.

Generally, I think more people are going to get published because there are a lot more small presses. These smaller presses are creating a wide range of possibilities for younger writers. A lot more work is going to come out. People are very prolific and very excited about writing right now.

c: What do you think about mainstream reviewers and native writing? Do you think they have the experience or the frame of reference to give meaningful reviews?

w: There's a big gap in some people's experience. One reviewer in Portland had talked about a poem I had written, "She's a Stranger to Intimacy." I don't really know who the persona was in the poem, but I thought she was a prostitute, an alcoholic, alone and alienated. The reviewer talked about her being an exotic dancer, but he didn't address the things in the poem that, to me, were the symbols of where the exploitation of women truly resides—in taboo, in religion, in issues of war.

The history behind that poem was my own coming to awareness of how women become who they are—what limitations that we impose on ourselves and accept. Not because the poem was a Native American poem, but because he didn't have the extra capacity or the compassion to investigate that, and so to him it was just an interesting poem about an exotic dancer.

c: Let's talk about poetry for a moment. The rhythm of poetry delivered in the poet's own voice has such a different impact. Do you think it's more meaningful when read aloud?

w: Yes, I do. I do that myself, with my own work and the work of others. As a reader I make all kinds of little mental skips. We're not taught how to read poetry. When I was in high school, I took a poetry class, which I failed. It didn't mean anything to me. We were studying John Donne and Middle English and Shakespeare, whom I now love. But it just didn't have the magic then. It wasn't until I read

Going for the Rain by Simon Ortiz that the magic of poetry made sense. And it wasn't because I understood it—I would just read and think this guy's talking about stuff that means something to me. I began to realize when I went to school down in Santa Fe, and Phillip Foss was talking about how a poem would look on the page; he would talk about craft; he would talk about line breaks, stanzas, and pauses, and the relationship of words sitting next to each other. We were "scoring" our work onto the page.

I had this class called "Ethno-poetics," which was wonderful. We studied *Beowulf* and *The Green Knight* and looked at the work in terms of it being ethnic poetry. I learned that poetry's origins go way back into religious ceremonial origins. It goes back to the origins of ourselves. It goes back to the way the land shapes how we hear things, how we sense time. We talked about the aboriginal people and how when two people met each other they would recite thousands and thousands of lines of poetry that was basically their lineage. It wasn't until years later, kind of by osmosis, that I incorporated all this into my work.

c: What about long-range plans?

w: One part of it is to keep writing short stories. I'd like to have a collection of that work at some point. I've been kind of shoved into essay writing, so I'm going to have to tune that up a bit more. I would like to write novels, which means I would have to have more time. I think the only thing that has ever worked for me is to make it my life to do it, and somehow it all falls into place.

I wrote *Hand into Stone* when I got out of school at the Institute of American Indian Arts and at Portland State. I studied with Henry Carlile and Primus St. John. I came home, and my mom graciously let me live with her for a few months. She let me use her old black Royal typewriter on this teeny stand, and she let me write and type. I sold blood and plasma at the Plasma Center and got food stamps and eventually moved into government-subsidized housing. [*Laughs*] That was my fellowship. [*Laughs harder*] Poverty enabled me to write that book! That and not having a job, because I didn't have any skills. So, I definitely don't want to go that route again. I don't have the energy for that.

You know I talked about poverty, but my aunt Lillian [Pitt] has been a major support to me in my writing and in my life. For years she has given me employment when she needed help and I needed a job. She has given me a sense of stability and has taught me to be independent. I have a lot of ongoing gratitude for my aunt Lillian. And I have learned to adjust my lifestyle so I can write.

c: What words would you like to share with beginning and emerging writers?

w: Writing is a natural thing. As writers, when we go to school, we are in the process of learning and making adjustments to write what is naturally our own way of writing. Reading is essential. If you read the best, you're going to write better. When I say "the best," it doesn't necessarily mean what someone else calls the best. If you read what turns you on, you're going to write better. And practice. Writing is basically the art of practice. There are these tools and how-to books, but basically they're just triggers. If you want to take exercises and write cutesy poems and clever poems, that's perfectly all right. If you want to write something that makes people's hair stand on end, you write from the gut. If you want to write something that will give your audience enough energy to keep on going, then you have to come from the heart.

NORMAN GUARDIPEE

Do you see that broken circle?
Do you see the charred fragments?
Put it together, put it together.
Do you see the tree of life
withering in the middle?
Do you see the vision melting away?
Tell me if you see these things.
Tell me I'm not going crazy.

Norman Guardipee (1993)

Norman Guardipee was born and raised on the Blackfeet Indian Reservation in Browning, Montana. The middle son of Leann and Stanley
Guardipee, he has faced the same challenges as many reservation
youth, including trouble with drugs and alcohol and living far from
home and family in an Indian boarding school. He has faced loneliness
and the ongoing struggle for identity and direction, especially after his
father's death in 1981.

A developing visual artist and writer, Guardipee graduated with
honors from Chemawa Indian School in Salem, Oregon, shortly before
this 1994 conversation and was planning to attend the University of
Lethbridge in Alberta. He has made a commitment to the well-being of
the People and has provided thoughtful and articulate interview re-
sponses.

E. K. CALDWELL: How did you decide to attend Chemawa?
NORMAN GUARDIPEE: The summer I got out of junior high I started to
    experiment with drinking and marijuana. I started getting into a lot
    of trouble. My mom finally told me she thought I should go to board-

ing school and get straightened up. I agreed because I was afraid I was going to end up another statistic on the rez, like maybe get killed or something because of the drinking and stuff.

c: What was it like for you when you left home?

g: I still remember the day because it was the saddest day of my life. I had never been away from my family, and I remember getting on the bus behind the police station, and my mom and sister were crying. I was really sad, and my mom was crying so hard she had to turn her back towards me. It felt like I was being kicked away and abandoned. I felt lost. My first few days at school I just laid in my room and thought about home.

   Then, as I started to know more people, I really got used to the school and actually started to like it, kinda like a whole new world. It was pretty much effort on my part to make me stay at Chemawa.

c: You mentioned that you considered your upbringing to have been traditional.

g: Pretty much. Dad used to sweat a lot. I was also raised Catholic. But I was just a little kid and didn't know much about things. I used to go out to my cousin's house. His grandfather is Buster Yellow Kidney. That's who showed me the most about traditional life. I am really grateful for that. That was my favorite place to go because I could escape out there. Everybody was traditional, and they all cared about one another. When I got to Chemawa, I always tried to go and sweat because it helped me stay at school.

c: What was going on with you when you decided to start drinking?

g: I think that's when I was lost. My mom didn't like it, and she would always bawl me out. I found out later that I'm actually allergic to alcohol, so that didn't make it any easier. Now I've been sober about two and a half years. I didn't drink or smoke any weed at school, but when I would go home, I would get into the old habit and go out looking for whatever I could get my hands on. Buster pulled me out of that whole cycle, and I'm really grateful to him. We need more people like him.

c: We have heard many stories about the awful experience of being in the Indian boarding schools. You spent four years at Chemawa. What do you think about the whole idea of these kinds of schools?

g: They can have a good purpose. Many times they lose their grasp of what they're supposed to be doing—which is educating Indian students. Educating them in the right way. They don't use fair discipline, and they just confuse a student with how unfair their discipline is. They also have a tendency to squander the money that is essential to provide the things we need for our education in a boarding school. And they don't want to have to answer to anybody, especially the students, for how they spend the money. They may have good intentions, but like they say, "The road to hell is paved with good intentions." [*Laughs*] A lot of times they just think crazy. It gets really hard to learn because of something a teacher is doing and especially the things administrators do. [*Pauses*] Maybe they don't know who they really are in their own identity, and they pass that confusion on to others.

c: What do you think are the essential ingredients for good education?

g: A lot of kids have it hard. They don't really learn well out of books. I know I don't learn that well out of books, but I learn enough to pass the course. But if they show you something, so your eyes can see it, then you can really learn it. Indian students in general can learn better like that.

c: Are there many Indian teachers at Chemawa?

g: A few, but they're not the majority at all.

c: Do you think the schools would be more effective if the teachers were Indian?

g: Yeah, I think so. I can get along okay with the white teachers, but Indian students like myself will always feel more comfortable with Indian teachers.

c: What will you study in college?

g: Philosophy. I really like that. Philosophy, I think, is what brings a lot of people out of chaos, out of hatred and anger towards one another.

It really helps. It's hard sometimes to talk philosophy with people because they think you're preaching to them, when you're really just talking about other options and other ways to look at something.

C: How would you define your philosophy?

G: You should live a good life and try to be good to everyone and try to help them. Be good to yourself and your body and remember that life is a gift and we can't really afford to squander it. Every morning I get up and pray to Creator and thank him for the new day and seeing the light again. When the sun goes down in the west every night, I always pray because that might be the last time you see that sun. If at the end of the day I am no longer here, then I pray that I have lived good up until my time to leave. That's my philosophy.

C: How is your philosophy reflected in your writing?

G: A lot of it talks about spirituality and culture. That poem I did about the broken circle suggested to me what I felt in my heart and the feelings other people have in their hearts. Because the circle has been around for thousands of years, and now it's come apart because people are forgetting about the ways of the spirit and the ways of kindness to people. They're greedy and money hungry and want power, and that won't do much when they get to the spirit world. What the poem suggests is that if people's visions vanish and our way of life isn't like a growing, healthy tree, then we will all vanish. One of the reasons I write and do art is to put emphasis on my culture.

People need to learn why they're doing what they're doing, like why you're dancing a powwow dance or singing some song and see the strength in it. And see the pity, yeah, the pity of the culture. All of that is in there. The sadness, the heartbreak, the broken promises, and so are the rewards and the miracles. Or even in a hug from a person who really loves you. That's powerful. That's the philosophy of Indian life. It is centered around the spirits and around the Creator. All of it. You make prayer the basis of your life. The kids need to learn this now. They can't stick with these stereotypes of Indians as drunks or as stupid or every beat-up car being a rez car. If you could measure wealth in terms of how we were before the white man came, and put that in modern-day terms, geez, we'd be the richest people. And then they'd say, "Look at that rez car," and a BMW would go flying by! [*Laughs*] They associate so many stereotypes with dirtiness and stupidity. That's not how we are. The romantic version of us is just as bad.

A real warrior is loving and kind to his people, and a lot of times kids don't see it. I know it's deep in their hearts, and they need people to show them what it means. We have to get out of that John Wayne tough man kind of thing. Like that thing about "real men don't cry." Indians believe you have to cry. I know in ceremonies I've seen the old men, they cry. It's so pitiful yet so life renewing. I feel it in my heart when I see the elders cry for the People.

c: What do you think are the biggest challenges for young Indian people?

g: One of the biggest challenges is the alcohol and drugs. We have to get away from that. Another thing is spiritual genocide, like with this so-called New Age Movement. This is one of the biggest challenges I know I personally have to face. A lot of non-Indians are running sweat lodges and doing Sun Dances, which I find totally unacceptable. It really hurts me to see them doing this. I'm not saying non-Indians shouldn't go to sweats. A true sweat leader will not kick someone out because they're not Indian. But they shouldn't be running ceremonies and acting like they have the right to sell our ways.

To run ceremonies has a different kind of power. A lot of people misunderstand and get into this control thing that is dangerous and hurts people. They'll get up on that pedestal and think everybody's below them. When we sit in that circle, that represents that everybody's equal and you need to have everybody praying with you. A lot of times they make Indian spirituality really complex, but it's really simple. They want to make it into this giant stereotype of Indians.

People who run ceremonies and charge money are giving this fake philosophy and this pale image of the Indian way. That's why the people who use it get even more lost. For people to take sacred objects and start selling them like candy bars, well, then it has no deep meaning, and it pretty much has no spirit.

Another challenge right now is the big issue about blood lines. There's talk on my rez about lowering the blood quantum so more people can be enrolled. I don't know how I stand on that. I'm over half myself, but I'm also part white. There are people who want the blood quantum so low that people who just think they're Indian might show up and get enrolled. I don't want that.

In 1975, when I was born, that didn't seem to be an issue. Nobody cared if you were half- or full-blood or whatever. But now it's like Indian against Indian, and that's no good at all. What I think is Indian is what's in your heart, and it's in your blood, too, but you don't have to have blood quantums. You either are Indian or not. It turns us against one another deciding who's the "most" Indian.

People might be saying a lot of bad things about each other now, but sometime later they will go to those same people for help. Usually people won't respond with kindness and will put them out, and that just makes the cycle go on and on. We need to break that cycle. We have to.

There are a lot of frauds out there. But we know the Creator won't let them run it all out. They will lose their path on it. They always end up going a different way.

c: When you think about your future, what do you see?

G: I don't know yet. I want to get as much knowledge as I can. I see a really sad time coming for lots of people, and I want to be there to help them in some way. I hope I make a difference somehow. After studying philosophy, maybe I'll go into counseling, like drug and alcohol counseling for Indian people my age and even younger. I want to be able to show people there is at least a glimmer of hope if we pull together.

RICK BARTOW

Artist Rick Bartow has created a body of work in the past decade that absorbs the viewer into a visceral journey. It is a journey of transition and transformation, imbued with what his people, the Polikla (Yurok), call *niwo*, "the spirits that are everywhere and are in everything." It is an ancient fusion of human relationship with the natural world. Bartow's unique contemporary style, saturating color and form, creates images that arrest the viewer, generating emotion that ranges from the raw and disturbing to the exquisitely tender and compassionate. His work is internationally appreciated and has received recognition and awards. This conversation focuses on his artistic process.

E. K. CALDWELL: Many articles have focused on your history and how the depth of your personal pain has influenced your work. You said you're tired of it. That makes sense considering your own evolution as a person and an artist.

RICK BARTOW: One of my favorite analogies of living is about [how] somebody takes a poop on the trail, and then every day they step in it. Then someone says to them, "Do you need to step in it everyday?" For me, as a recovering alcoholic and as a crazy artist and a Nam vet, it's also something to be aware of because we can allow things to happen to us by dragging it to us repeatedly. So, you talk about those things, and after a period of time, move on. But they're always with me. It's like the poop on the trail—it's there, and I can either step in it, or hop around it, or make a new trail. And I was blessed in my life to be given enough room to have a new trail. It's as simple as that.

C: Good, then let's talk about your work. How would you describe your own artistic process?

B: Art is real intuitive. I start with just a smear on the paper and start erasing with what I call "cutting into it," making marks into that area or smearing it with my hands. It's a very physical process, art. A lot of people think of art as being very genteel. Not so with me. I really get in there and sweat, and after a point, I bleed. My fingertips get worn away, because of the smudging. And I haven't been able to break that habit. I've bought the paper tools to blend, and it doesn't do it. Skin on the paper is what does it. I get to that bleeding point, and I have to stop for a little while and look at things and let my fingertips rest. So, I work from that intuitive place of just making random marks, blobs of color, and seeing what shapes present themselves.

Early on I did a picture where there was a dog fight. Animals fight with every atom and particle of their being. Except I do it in nursery colors like pinks and baby blues, mauves and real light colors. To do a factual rendering of that, well, that's been done by somebody. Or I could take a photo of dogs fighting, but it just doesn't interest me. I use whatever I can to get you to stop and look. Erase part of the face or give it three eyes or take the nose off or leave the head out, or whatever I can to get you to stop and look and absorb a little more. You can hardly think of anything new. That's why I have to work the way I do—because I am painfully aware that I am not unique.

I also do what I call "mining." Going into the studio and doing the dots and the lines and the smears and erase and cut out, and then something will happen and I'll get something—an image. There's blind response to line and color and form—there's always this panic—the panic of tabula rasa, and I'm going to fill the void, and how do you do that? But work, that's the magic thing, and it takes us to that place where everything just feels right. It requires every day, just doing something. If nothing else, just go in there and clean up the studio, and then if something happens, you'll be ready.

I work the way I do so that I don't sully, slander, or wish to come close to native artists who are very traditional in their approach. I know that way is long and narrow and very hard. It takes part of your life to do it. I've only done it a couple times in a very minimal way, and that was enough to show me that it is something unto itself, and you don't mess with it. Like some of these people with "Shaman #3," or "Myodor the Odiferous Coming Out of the Ground," or whatever, well, you can have it. Because in creating those kinds of things, Myodor the Odiferous might just come right out of the ground, and I don't want to be in your shoes when he does. There are some things you just shouldn't be messing with, especially if you're not willing to take on all that goes with it.

c: Critics have identified "movement" as the fundamental principle upon which your work is based. Is the focus shifting in your work from the personal to more universal kinds of themes?

b: The first group of work was a series of single images, and then the series where there were masks falling away, stripping away all these fearful things like self-loathing. Some of them were autobiographical and some less so. I don't think that you can entirely divorce yourself from it, like some of these people who can take one video camera and point it at another one and call that art. I'm having a lot of trouble with the art world these days and what they call "flash art." Well, I don't get it. And nobody can explain it to me, because to me the craft is out of it. As I realized more that I could no longer see myself as the center of the universe, and I was only a part of the universe, then the images began to change. Lots of things started happening on the paper because I wasn't just a "me," I was an "us."

c: Where do you see the work moving?

b: Cleaning up. That's so damn much more fun than being crazy and being sick. Now I can be afraid, and I can banish fear with truth or with trying, and if I fail, I realize I tried.

c: In this recent group of work, what is there that you particularly like?

b: There was a real strange skeleton figure with hearts and things called *Chet Baker*, the jazz trumpet player, who to me embodies everything my art does. He was a raging junkie maniac, and then on the other side of him was this guy who sang "My Funny Valentine" with this real lady-killing voice. It's kind of like the art. There's a lot of pretty things there, but they come from a not so pretty place sometimes. The piece for Chet Baker is about mortality. I like to think about what the old guys used to say about, "No death, only a change of place." The healing of grief is part of transformation.

I actually drew a figure with clothes on. [*Laughs*] Shocking. I guess I drew nude people because when you clean up you also have to deal honestly with people who are living human beings. And you are naked and with *you*, and what happens is remarkable, because in the end you look, and it's just you. There's no great lesion where your heart should be, and you're grateful. There are several in this batch called *Relationship*—one of a woman in a low-back dress, and you see the other person there, who is neither male nor female. I just leave it open and do what I do the best I can do it, you know.

C: Any idea what happened to give permission to put clothes on the figures?

B: Maybe it's too new for me to assimilate what's going on. Actually, it might have to do with clothing yourself in belief, in prayer. How you clothe yourself and protect yourself with that.

C: In one of the articles I read, it said that the arcs, the crosses, the dotted lines, all imply the life force.

B: It comes up a lot—"Well, what about the crosses? Is that Christian?" And I say, "No." The cross to me is like the ultimate humiliation of western man—of taking one man and saying he is the cause of all of it, and then nailing him up to torture him. Whoever knocked those nails in, well, I doubt if their family is still happy because I doubt they could ever get away from something like that. In truth, in my work, if that cross means anything, it is a visual symbol of prayer in the four directions.

C: What kind of working environment do you need to have?

B: Kind of quiet, but then I might make it noisy by playing tapes really loud. Music, poetry, mythology, and old photographs all inspire me. I like it a little warm, and I usually work in a really small space. I have one now that is 12′ by 9′, and I had trouble back there. I got so close to the wall [*laughing*] that my nose was doing more smudging than my fingers because I felt so insecure with all that room around me.

c: How's your working rhythm?

b: Really, I'm spastic. It used to be that I did my best work between nine and midnight. Now I'm working from late morning to late afternoon. Then I'll knock off and go for a walk. In the old studio I worked at night more. This one's cooler at night and bigger, and I work better there during the day. Last year I would have told you just the opposite.

c: Do you think that has anything to do with shift in the work itself?

b: Could be. But I don't really know. I'm not terribly introspective. [*Laughing*] I'm more retrospective. The way I work doesn't depend on natural light. I work under bulbs and tubes. I'd probably feel much less inhibited if I didn't have any windows in the studio at all. So, those kinds of things don't really influence the work.

c: What about when you get immobilized and feel you can't work?

b: Generally, I feel like it's not from lack of things to work on but the advent of too many ideas. It requires a discipline that I sometimes don't employ, like, "Okay, today I'm going to work on sculpture." I have to do it all at once. Generally when I feel that block and can't work, I'm looking maybe on the inside of my eyelids, or maybe I'm reading poetry or looking at the images of the old photographs, and I'm "mining" again. It might not be the image so much but how something technical works with the image. Suddenly something will come back to me, like this shape with that or something flat with something glossy or breaking it up a certain way. This helps me not stay frozen up because I'll just go back in and work it and not worry about it. I used to worry if I felt blocked. Now I don't. Some Chinese philosopher said, "A day spent in contemplation is not a loss." Sometimes you have to shut down for a little while in terms of the external work. Once I shut down for more than a certain length of time, there are too many possibilities. Then it's time for me to limit them to one specific area. That's where discipline comes in, and it's discipline of a nature that we don't often think about. It's more like a spiritual discipline to start out the day with a prayer and to finish it with a prayer.

I know how to work. Sometimes I don't get up off [my butt] to go to the studio and unlock the door and turn on the radio and put up a piece of paper and sit there and look at it. There are times when I know that I'm going to ruin what I'm doing. Now I'm pretty well able to shut that off. I know there are some things that are hopeless—get some images going, and I know that it's a piece of crap, and there's no sense working on it, but I'll work on it another hour and then throw it away. But even that is working. That's like putting in the time and just being in there for it to happen. Inspiration accounts for so little. It's wonderful—don't get me wrong. But it accounts for so little that it's hardly worth mentioning.

c: How are the various mediums interrelated in the rhythm of your work?

b: Well, they all go hand in hand. The drawing leads to the painting leads to the sculpture leads to the print and the carving. They all seem to interact at some point like living interacts with art, and you just can't separate too many things apart. It's real unremarkable from my point of view. Generally what you discover when you are fortunate enough to work in more than one medium is that sometimes if it isn't happening for you in one place, then you might be able to work it out in one of the others.

c: What words or thoughts would you have for young people that are being drawn towards the arts?

b: When you make a mark, you're the only one that can make that mark, and don't let someone tell you that you're wrong for doing it, because you're the only one that can do it your way. I've been given many blessings, all because of making marks on paper. Through the arts it's possible to have this wonderful life that I call my own now. It's also not that big a blessing that it couldn't happen to you. The one thing that underlies all of this is friends. My friends and my family always had courage and confidence in me. I also have to say that a spiritual belief is important. I don't think any of this is by accident. I don't say that anyone else has to believe this. That's just me talking for myself. There's no reason why you can't have an art career. And, yes, you have to lead with your heart, but you also have to learn how to be a professional. If you're going to be out there in the marketplace, there are certain rules you have to know about. That doesn't mean you have to follow them to the letter, but you do have to approach the marketplace with some of the rules intact.

I think that for anybody involved in the arts, that it's a valid way to go. Art is universal, and it may go even beyond that. Art is like medicine—good medicine because it helps you as you create it, and it helps others as they experience it. And it can go way beyond your lifetime. I'm my son and my grandson and so forth. What I leave behind for them, well, I don't want no hokey-jokey two computers looking at each other. I can't go with that. I want them to know something about what I believed in, and part of that is what I put down. If you're creating art and taking responsibility for your art, you will be protected and taken care of by it. One thing that's a given when you're doing art is that *you're doing art*. A friend of mine from Seattle and I were talking when the market was really dismal (and I was praying to the bank instead of to the Creator), and he reminded me that we had already been blessed today because we were both still artists.

BONNIE BLACKWOLF

It was the early 1990s when the telephone rang in a house by the river on Oregon's Mt. Hood, and Bonnie Blackwolf, already ill with hepatitis B, was informed by an infectious disease specialist that she was HIV positive. "I was real sick," commented the Blackfeet woman three years later, "but I managed to get out of bed and throw some things around. I was full of rage and anger and felt abandoned. I was forced into looking at my own mortality." She had begun getting tested every six months nearly five years earlier, after she began her sobriety. She recognized the onset of the hepatitis as a potential precursor to HIV/AIDS, and she requested another HIV test. Blackwolf credits her foundation in sobriety through twelve-step programs with helping her avoid relapse into drug and alcohol addiction upon learning of her HIV positive diagnosis. About a year and a half prior to the interview she was diagnosed with AIDS. "When I first got sober I would say that if I ever got AIDS, I would go right out and shoot some dope because I'm going to die anyway. And what I've learned over time is that the freedom I feel in abstinence from alcohol and drugs is the best thing I could have."

Her journey in dealing with AIDS continued to take her through many transitions in her internal landscape and also resulted in her efforts to educate others about HIV/AIDS. She spoke at high schools, treatment centers, and community gatherings and to individuals. Blackwolf also did radio interviews and worked with the Portland-based nonprofit organization PEACE (Protection of Earth, Animals, Children, and Elders), which raises money for activism related to Indian issues, and later with Planet Peace, an Internet project for the distribution of information regarding indigenous and environmental causes.

Bonnie Blackwolf died from HIV/AIDS in December 1997.

E. K. CALDWELL: How did you make your decision to become so active and visible in terms of HIV/AIDS?

BONNIE BLACKWOLF: I knew how important it was to see others out in the world functioning and doing things. I needed to do that, and when I did that as a woman I did not find the support. I met many people infected with HIV/AIDS, but no women. I needed that peer support desperately. Fortunately, I had networks around the country, and I knew of women in other places that I could call. I knew that it was important that we start breaking down the epidemic of fear, because I know that the epidemic of fear is much more dangerous than the disease. And that if we hate ourselves enough, we will truly stop living. That's what the epidemic of fear perpetrates.

I also know that people who have been long-term survivors with AIDS have worked with others. I get to look at the people I know today and see how they live and how they feel, and I know that it's okay for me to have dreams again. I thought all that stopped and that I couldn't pursue anything because I was going to die. It's taken me three years to get it—that I deserve to live. I deserve to be loved and to love other people, and I deserve to have dreams.

That epidemic of fear told me that it was not okay and not acceptable to have dreams and be loved if you have AIDS. The fear is perpetrated by the church and perpetrated by assimilated people who don't have a connection to the source. They don't understand that this is a grain of sand on the beach compared to the big picture of things. It's that big picture that lets me know that we're carrying messages here. And it's not about, "Oh, poor Bonnie's going to die, and that's the end of it, and poor me, and get me another drink." It's about carrying messages so that the mother can be supported in her healing. So we can heal our blood lines and go to the source of what we know and remember who we are. When fear knocks me out of my body, I don't have a clue about who I am. People need to know that we're out there so they have somewhere to go and know they are not alone with this. Because we'll go underground. We'll hibernate till we die. I've heard stories of people who go off into the hills and live by themselves and die, and no one has even been told that this has happened to them.

c: In terms of support from the people around you, how has that been for you since your diagnosis and in dealing with the disease?

b: Initially, people that I least expected to be there were, and the people that I thought would be there weren't. I didn't tell my family until last year. They acted really unaffected, which was real hard. What they say is, "Of course, if she's gay, she's got to have AIDS," which is a real homophobic perspective.

c: How do you see the homophobia in our communities being part of the epidemic of fear?

b: We have used the epidemic of fear and the conditioning of non-Indian culture to turn on each other. What is that about? A lot of people believe in their hearts that gayness is not okay. But how can we talk out one side of our mouths about respecting all forms of life, but when it comes to gay people, it's not okay. Are we not a form of life?

At a gathering I went to, one of the things that was impressive to me was women from all kinds of perspectives shared their pain, and people sat and listened to that pain, regardless of the woman's background. From that we were able to see how we had been separated and what we needed to be aware of with each other to come together. We all had different realities, but those could coexist and come together for a different picture. One of the things that I talked about was, "Why is it that our gay people are not at this gathering, and why are we not talking about their absence? Why aren't we talking about AIDS?"

After that gathering I had five women come up to me and talk about their gay son or daughter or having a grandson who died of AIDS. Why aren't gay people at those gatherings? Because we don't feel welcome. It is not safe for us to do that. I hear many stories about gay people growing up on the reservations and then leaving and getting AIDS and coming back home to die. And people don't know what to do with them. There are traditional people who have taken their children for healing in their ways, and that is good. We need to take a look at how we're going to reach people. If you have a teenage son who comes to you and says, "I'm HIV positive," and he also happens to be gay, what will you do? If you turn your back on him, then he's one more seventh-generation child, lost. You can blame that on a system, or you can embrace him and tell him that you love him.

I heard a story about one young man who was diagnosed HIV positive and, for whatever reason, was unable to go to his family and tell them. He ended up hanging himself in a hotel room. He may not have done that had he not been so frightened and alone. When I look at that picture, I say to myself, "What is wrong with us?" We have to look at how we treat one another. Are we treating one another like our perpetrators have treated us? We all do that. I've done it, and I don't have a right to do that.

The homophobia issue is very controversial, and I don't have anything to lose, so I'm going to keep talking about it. If I have to die talking about it, well, I've been beaten within an inch of my life for being gay. It's another level of fear in operation. We don't have the right to beat on one another on any level for any reason. The way we get AIDS is through behavior. It's not about being shameful in the eyes of God because we're gay. It's not about punishment, and it's not about that we've been bad human beings who deserve to die this terrible suffering death. We have to stop buying into the predator conditioning of identifying risk groups instead of risk behaviors. It's not who we are, it's what we do that will determine if we get this disease. It's really sad when we're trying to fill up that void. We're trying to find that love and belonging. When we're in pain and want to be loved, it's like, "In this moment, in this night, in my drunkenness, if somebody shows me something that looks like it might be about loving me for one minute, then I don't care if I get thrown off a cliff five minutes later because I get to have that, and I get to feel that for a moment." What is it in us that has been taught that love is supposed to be like that? There's so much more to love than sex.

c: How did you deal with people withdrawing from you?

b: I was hurt, but I understood it. What was real clear to me in the beginning was that dealing with what this means is to be alone on some level in terms of my own healing and coming to some peace within myself about it. At that time I was so sick with hepatitis that I was delirious, and I was fighting demons was what I was doing. I was making another soul or spirit decision to live at that point. There were a series of days when I was by myself. Fortunately, I was up by the river and the mountain in this great house, so environmentally I had a lot of support, but I had to make a decision to live, and that was a real personal thing between myself and Creator. I had to make that choice to open up to the love and the giving of others to keep my body on the planet at that point. I couldn't hit the wall anymore and believe that I could get up and do it again. That's how I had lived my whole life. That was no longer an option, and that scared me. I didn't know how to be gentle with myself, and I didn't know how to allow myself to be loved. I got to learn about that. Now it never stops. Basically, I was learning about stopping the war inside myself. I was very confused about how to accept that this has happened and surrender to being open to learn more. And at the same time fight the disease in order to stay alive.

I know that there is not anything on this earth that occurs that cannot be healed. That's a contradiction in terms when you look at the statistics. Daily I hear about someone who has passed over or is dying or who is real sick with AIDS. When I look at that, I know that we're not there yet. I realized what I was afraid of down the line was the suffering, not the dying. I had a lot of experiences where I almost died, and overdoses where I did die and came back, and so the dying's not it. I know that's a wonderful place to be. But I also know right now I want to be here, and there are things I understand a little better. I'm learning there are things I have to do that aren't done yet.

c: What are you seeing in terms of people's response to the messages you carry? Especially the young people.

B: I think that because of my history, people hear some of what I say. People seem to get educated once someone they know and care about has the disease. It's unfortunate that we have to get hit over the head.

I don't think that my message in dealing with young people is close enough to home. I think the peer message, other young people who are infected and who are talking about their lives, is reaching people more. This generation of young people is looking at the full spectrum of genocide. It's like, "What do we have to live for?" A lot of young people don't want to hear it anymore, because it's one more level of hopelessness. It's one more thing that might kill us, so what? There is so much pain in even being on the planet now, and to survive we have to keep functioning. To be inundated by the fear and the pain is a very hopeless place to be. How do we get out of that sense of hopelessness?

C: With education and prevention, what do you think works?

B: In the face of this industrial madness, we have to have levels of self-determination amongst our own people. To bring that cultural experience back into play is so hard. We're talking about picking up all the sticks. Traditionally, we knew who we were. We were shown who we were. We were taught who we were, and are. We had a place of importance, and we had every reason to believe, because we had our communities around us. We had every reason to know deep inside of us that we were worth something, and we could believe what we were told.

I know we're working in that direction. I see people working at doing that, and I'm grateful that it's going on. There are some young people who are looking at that, and I think the young people who are being born now, they know more already than we know. They came here knowing what they're walking into, and they're not as willing to forget about it. We can't be separated and isolated and in prisons and hospitals and dead. We sacrifice the children every time we do that. Because if it's not AIDS, then what else is it going to be? I don't buy the green monkey theory. To me, AIDS is clearly a tool of genocide. Knowing what we know, we've got to be responsible about choices that we make, and make choices that don't endanger ourselves and our own people.

C: How were you affected by seeing people with HIV/AIDS becoming visible in the media?

B: I felt some sense of support, like being a part of the design in the beadwork, and that I wasn't completely alone. People have been forced to be warriors on their own, in spite of how we're treated on a day-to-day basis by health care and by our own families, and learning that we have a responsibility to the people out there. I knew that I had a responsibility to be visible because we have to depend on ourselves to educate ourselves. We can't depend on the so-called authoritarian figures to give us right information. It is not in their best interest to do that.

In the media there is this level of sensationalism or romance with how visibility is portrayed. There was a well-educated woman who became infected after one sexual encounter with a man. You would see big articles on her here and there. They did what people generally do with Indian women, and it was like, "Look at this strong and powerful Indian woman," which happens to be true, except that their perceptions of who that woman really is and what she goes through are very misguided and unclear. They're reinforcing the system that set her up to be misunderstood, which leaves out all of who we are. If we start talking about who she is, and what she feels and needs, and how she's been mistreated and hurt, then they can't relate to that. I don't think anybody who gets a diagnosis is all at peace and cool about the whole thing.

Someone who already has a high media profile, like Magic Johnson, had a very powerful impact on the whole country. It really got people's attention. But he comes from a place of economic privilege, and that's a more comfortable place to come from, especially to a national television audience, compared to being an Indian woman with children who's maybe by herself and feels like she has the flu, and she has to think, "So what, I've always got the flu, and I've got these kids, and I've got to do this and do that." She doesn't have the options. She can't sit on some program where there's all this hope and support, saying "I'm going to live a long time and rah, rah, rah."

The truth is that most people of color who are living inside economic oppression end up in the hospital with full-blown AIDS and have a life expectancy of something under a year. We don't get the intervention that we need, whatever that looks like. I was resentful, and I didn't want to hear about Magic's thirty-million-dollar bank account. It's like—that's real good for you, but why isn't somebody we know sitting there talking about growing up in a system that's tried to kill me and my family my whole life. This is what it feels like. People have good hearts, and they want to educate, and I understand that. But they need to identify the conditioning of the system and how that affects people.

c: Have you now established a support system here in the city with other women who are HIV positive or have AIDS?

b: Actually, no. In Portland my support system, in terms of people living with AIDS, is men. I have met and correspond with other women who are living with AIDS in other parts of the country. In terms of Indian women living here, they are not coming forward. That's been hard. Real hard. I've done radio interviews and written ads and whatever, and I don't know another Indian woman living with AIDS in Portland. I know of them, but we have not been introduced.

It saddens me, because I think it's another symptom of the epidemic of fear that these women don't feel safe enough, and I understand that. Our lives are on the line. In the Indian community a lot of people go underground if they test positive, or we're not getting tested because we're afraid or those services are not available. We don't like labels. Labels have kept us oppressed through the mental health system for a very long time, so the last thing we're going to do is go into an all-white agency. I don't know any Indian person who hasn't lost people in their family due to diseases brought to this country. If we're going to get real about what our needs are with non-Indian people, we don't have any reason to believe that something will be not be taken from us, be it our children, or our dignity, or any number of things.

C: Have you had any experience with Indian Health Services, and has that experience been equally distressing?

B: I had some contact in other states. I saw another epidemic of fear, and people were not treated right. Indian Health, for a lot of reasons we already know, is not able to provide the resources and the needed care. That's very distressing. There isn't a lot of prevention effort going on. The needs of Indian people are not being met. I saw people treated really unfairly within their own communities. They lost their jobs, their anonymity was broken, and the community knew they had AIDS before they did. It's a classic story, and we need to understand that one more time, in the AIDS epidemic, we're trying to kill each other, and the system doesn't have to because we're doing it to each other.

C: When you look at the reality of the faulty research and how little information has been gathered about the effects of this disease on our people, plus the general lack of research on women . . .

B: Right. Genocide comes in a lot of forms.

C: It seems like people more easily accept others having the disease when they look "normal" and are asymptomatic. Would you talk about the difference in response when people become symptomatic?

B: Unless you have been around people who have AIDS, when you see a positive asymptomatic individual out there educating and doing things, I think it reinforces the denial. It's like, "Well, gee, they seem okay, and they don't seem to be suffering." Most of us don't want people to suffer. It's so heavy when you start to get sick—other people's own mortality is confronted. They don't want you to die. *They* don't want to die. It's very frightening. It means that the reality of the disease is coming in on them. Most people who have unresolved grief issues around losing someone close to them are not going to be available to you on a deep level because they are being restimulated by that old wound. People don't get close to you because they're afraid of losing, and I understand that. There are healthy boundaries around that. But I think running from the reality of life and death doesn't work. The assimilated culture of America has never had a clue about dealing with the transition of living and dying. That's the fear, and it's worked very well. The hand of the system is very effective again when we believe and live in that manner.

Another part of it is needing to be touched and held. People don't believe people who have AIDS or are HIV positive should be in sexual relationships. (I don't think you'll find many people who will be honest enough to tell you that. Because what is politically correct is to say, "Well, sure. Go ahead. There's safe sex and whatever.") One more time you end up feeling alone and ashamed. In my most distraught moments, I sometimes have this feeling like my body is rotting, and there's nothing I can do. Like it's slowly and gradually fizzling into this nothingness. When you need to be held, and you need to be close to someone, you need to be reminded of who you are as spirit. When people are so caught up in their own fear, I feel ripped off and angry. The gift that [AIDS] gives me is that I get to become empowered and real clear about what my wants and needs are. And [laughs] I don't like that. I don't like having to say, "Look, I can't do that. I can't travel here or there. I can't stay up late. I can't do this because it will shorten my life span if I don't take care of myself." But people don't want to hear about it because it means there's going to be more death.

I also want to talk about the people who are incredible warriors. They are there. They know they are risking pain—they know what it looks like. They know it's going to be awful at some point in time, and they hang in there. Because they recognize the spirit in body, like one of those sayings that I've always loved, "We're spiritual beings having a human experience, not human beings having a spiritual experience." When I remember that, I'm okay. Those people who stand by you, they know that. Without those people, I wouldn't be here. I've had a lot of love given to me, and my concept of real love is different today. If I can open myself up to that, it's out there, and that love is what keeps us alive. It's respect and honor for all life. Truly getting it that we are all a part of this. The so-called darkness and the light, and the evil and the good, we are nothing without all those things. We have a responsibility to make sure that respect and honor endure so that we have a place to be.

c: Have you been able to access traditional medicine? Are you using any western medicines, or is it a combination of methods?

b: We can go to someone in a good way and ask for healing. It doesn't stop there. It's about every day and how we live and how we are. It's not going and saying, "Fix me," and it's over. It's a commitment to a way of living, and it's a challenge. That's part of that healing. I don't think dying is a failure. I believe what has been said, "Diseases can heal lives." Maybe the rest of your life is three days, but in that three days there is healing, and there is perspective, and there is reality. So to die is not to fail. I know that there are people who can get rid of this virus. But if you step out of balance and continue to live the way you were, it comes back. You have to learn to embrace the whole picture.

I went off all my medical drugs about nine months ago, and my whole quality of life changed. There are chemical drugs that are responsible for keeping people alive day to day. Everyone is different, and some things work for some and not for others. I am fortunate at this time that I don't have to make that choice about staying alive with that kind of chemical stimulus or protection in my body. I do homeopathic medicine now like herbs and teas. I sweat when I can, and I need to do that more. I think we have to be careful about the types of drugs that we choose to take because they use us as guinea pigs. The Centers for Disease Control used to be called the Tuskegee Institute. There is public information now that shows extensive biological warfare testing has gone on in the military. They have tested viruses in the subway systems of big inner cities and possibly the introduction of the AIDS virus through hepatitis B vaccines in the major cities in the country. This is the same organization that works with the World Health Organization. This is the same organization that now we know was involved in injecting pregnant women with plutonium. They were running tests on children who were so-called retarded who were not told what it was like to see in both worlds at the same time. And people say, "Oh, that's terrible! How could this happen?" Well, this is the same organization that we have lived with all these years. We have to be real careful about where we put ourselves.

c: Would you talk the about conscious preparation for the transition from life into death? Does it become a distraction in your thoughts?

b: It's about who we become when we know that our life may end sooner than we planned, and living life in this body today, as opposed to living years and years and then saying, "Oh, goodbye, you're out of here." To be conscious that this is a continuation. There are places that I'm going. There are things that are going to happen when I leave this body that are as important and as much a part of this whole creation as was my living here this time. Or life without a body. This is a universal support system. It's okay to think about it. I'm more comfortable with it now.

[*Pauses*] But, I'm always grateful when I have a day I don't think about it. When people pass over, you're reminded. I had a wonderful thing that happened. A man I knew of had come to a home to die, and the night that he passed over, he made a little sign and hung it on the door to his room. It said, "Do Not Disturb, Angel in Process." That really touched me. His understanding was so clearly conscious about recognizing himself as spirit. That eternal spirit. There was no question. I don't have any questions about whether there is a God, or worry that I may burn in hell. That's crap. That's predator conditioning. I have great comfort in knowing that understanding of spirit. It's unfinished business that I think about, the responsibilities I have to other people and the amends that need to be made, and I've worked on that. I try to encourage other people to not be afraid of conscious living and conscious dying.

Honestly, I think Indian people are a lot better about that. We recognize the truth in that passing and in that transformation. I feel sad for people [who] don't understand that and are afraid of it. I don't worry like I did. I worry when I don't feel well sometimes, though. I mean, the worse case scenario is being seventy pounds and in a bed, emaciated. Dimly lit room with [*laughs softly*] battleship grey walls with strange Hitchcock-looking nurses scurrying about and no one there and dying alone in some institution. That would be horrible. The truth for me today is that I know in my heart that it won't be like that. One of the things I have been taught by people who have passed over is that they have prepared. The preparation. That's what Indian people are taught their whole life—the importance of preparing in a good way to live and to leave. And if we'll remember that, we don't have to be afraid of dying.

SHERMAN ALEXIE

Pullman WA, 1989: A young premed student at Washington State University was in serious trouble with his chosen major. He was smart enough and had long considered himself a "science guy." But his equilibrium was giving him grief—he fainted three times in human anatomy class. To fill credits while contemplating a career change, he took a writing class. Five poems later, his instructor, Alex Kuo, asked him what he was doing with the rest of his life. The young man replied that he was "open to suggestion." Kuo had a suggestion. Writing. Fortunately for all of us, the young man said, "Okay, I'll be a writer."

Five years later, 1994: Twenty-seven-year-old Sherman Alexie, from the Spokane Reservation in Washington State, has published five books and has been called by the *New York Times* "one of the major lyric voices of our time." His first book, *The Business of Fancydancing* (Hanging Loose Press, 1992), was selected as the *New York Times Book Review* "1992 Notable Book of the Year." His second collection, *I Would Steal Horses* (1992), claimed first place in the fifth annual chapbook contest of Slipstream Press in Niagra Falls, New York. That same year Alexie was the recipient of a National Endowment for the Arts poetry fellowship. *Old Shirts and New Skins* (American Indian Studies Center, University of California, Los Angeles, 1993) and *First Indian on the Moon* (Hanging Loose Press, 1993; nominated for the Poetry Society of America's William Carlos Williams Award) next hit the presses. Then came the readings, securing an agent, and four rounds of bidding for his 1993 release *The Lone Ranger and Tonto Fistfight in Heaven* (nominated for the Pen/ Faulkner-Hemingway Award). Additional books appeared in subsequent years: *Reservation Blues* (Atlantic Monthly Press, 1995), *The Summer of Black Widows* (Hanging Loose Press, 1996), *Indian Killer* (Atlantic Monthly Press, 1996), and *Smoke Signals* (Hyperion, 1998). Alexie's heart has palpitated hard on more than one occasion, but his equilibrium seems to be in good shape. He hasn't fainted once.

E. K. CALDWELL: You have had amazing response to your work in a very short period of time. How are you dealing with that dramatic shift in rhythm?

SHERMAN ALEXIE: [*Laughing*] A shift in reality is what it is. It's not real, and it's not what matters. I think that I knew that from the beginning. Certainly there's a lot of hype and fireworks going on, but once the fireworks are over, you go home. It's a game, and I certainly don't take it seriously because the important thing I'm doing is affecting people's lives and getting stories told that aren't always heard. The rest of it is secondary.

C: How is all this traveling affecting the rhythm of your writing? How do you make time for new work?

A: I'm a binge writer anyway. When I'm home I'll write like ten or twelve hours a day for a couple weeks and catch up. I do write a lot of poems on the road, and most of what I write is fully written in my head before I ever put it on the page.

C: And they stay in your head without getting away from you?

A: Yeah, they do. I don't know exactly how I do that. I've always had a very good memory, and I can visualize the poems in my head and move things around. When it finally gets to the page, it's usually pretty good, and I don't have to do a lot of drafts. Sometimes not any drafts.

C: Reviewers say things like, "Well, this is life on the reservation." Do you think that your work really presents an accurate window of perception into life on the rez? Do you ever get concerned about people seeing it as perpetuating certain stereotypes?

A: I think the problem is that when people like me get all this attention, well, then people think that I'm telling the *only* truth. They get this idea that I'm the only image of life on a reservation and that what I'm saying is everything there is, but I'm just one set of eyes looking at my reservation and my own experience. I don't pretend to speak for all Indians. I don't pretend to speak for all the members of my tribe or my tribe itself. People place that upon me. To think that all Indian reservations are like that is not right at all. There are certainly common cultural things, functional and dysfunctional. And I don't believe that everyone's experience is like mine. I don't believe that, and I don't claim that.

C: How are the people from home responding to your work?

A: [*Laughs*] The people who didn't like me before still don't like me, and the people who liked me still do. I don't think it's really changed a lot. [*Laughing*] Although, I used to be one of those weak little Indian boys who got the crap kicked out of him by other Indian boys on a daily basis. And a lot of those people seem to have forgotten that they did that, and now they're all friendly, and I'm like, "Well, don't you remember that time you broke my nose? I do. I got a bump on my nose that I see in the mirror every day." I think that celebrity part of it can become where people are kind of sycophantic about it now. But, generally, I'm still just "Junior" out there, just like I've always been.

C: How are other established native writers who've been around, and still have not gotten the attention you're getting, responding to your work?

A: It's interesting, because the one I can think of who has been the most supportive has been writing longer than I have been alive. He has never gotten the kind of attention that his contemporaries have, and I'm not sure why because he's certainly as good a writer. That's Simon Ortiz. There is some sense of guilt at receiving this much attention, because I know that a big reason for my success is because other writers have come before, and their stories have done well. Leslie Marmon Silko, James Welch, Scott Momaday, Joy Harjo, and Simon are people who are my heroes. For me, especially at my age, I've already been places they haven't been and am getting closer to movie deals and levels they haven't been. I feel guilty in some sense, but I know also that every generation is supposed to move forward a little bit beyond what has already happened. They are the trailblazers.

And I'm taking it a little farther. Joy and Adrian Louis and Simon and Leslie are really supportive, sending encouragement and correspondence and responding to the work. I have become friends with others who are not as well known like Liz [Woody] and Vince [Wanassey] and Phil [Red Eagle]. Having that support of other people out there telling the stories is important to me, and I'm hoping my success will help my contemporaries.

c: Would you speak to what you see our responsibility being as native writers? Do you see that responsibility restricting or constricting certain avenues of creativity?

a: We do have a cultural responsibility above and beyond what other people do, more than other ethnic groups, simply because we are so misrepresented and misunderstood and appropriated. We have a serious responsibility as writers to tell the truth. And to act as (and I hate to use the word because people put it on me, and I don't like the responsibility) role models. We are more than just writers. We are storytellers. We are spokespeople. We are cultural ambassadors. We are politicians. We are activists. We are all of this simply by nature of what we do, without even wanting to be. So we're not like these other writers who can just pick and choose their expressions. They're chosen for us, and we have to be aware of that.

I also think we have a definite responsibility to live up to our words. As native writers, we can certainly talk the talk about the things that everybody should do and we should do, but if you're going to write about racism, I don't think you should be racist. If you're going to write about sexism and exploitation, then I don't think you should be sleeping around. If you're going to write about violence and colonialism, then I don't think you should be doing it to your own family. So, I think we have a serious responsibility as native writers to live traditionally in a contemporary world. And I don't think a lot of us do.

c: What do you think prevents us from doing that?

A: A lot of it is our own dysfunctions. While we may have more responsibility because of what we do, that does not automatically make us healthy. Part of the danger in being any artist of whatever color is that you have to fall in love with your wrinkles. The danger is that if you fall in love with your wrinkles, then you don't want to get rid of them. You start to glorify them and perpetuate them. If you write about pain, you can end up inevitably searching for more pain to write about, that kind of thing. That self-destructive route. We need to get away from that. We can write about pain and anger without having to let it consume us, and we have to learn how to do that in our lives as individuals before we can start doing it as writers.

C: What would you say to a young writer who is perhaps being drawn to write about something that is not typically perceived as "Indian"? Maybe some outrageous science fiction, and they are feeling, perhaps, that they aren't "allowed" to write about that because it doesn't have anything to do with what is currently perceived as "Indian"?

A: Well, I think that's great, as long as they make their characters Indians. I'd love to see Indian science fiction where you have Indians a hundred years from now, and they're riding in spaceships. I think that would be wonderful. As writers, though, I think whatever we do ends up being autobiography. If you start writing things too far removed from yourself, it's not going to be good. I mean those young writers who want to write science fiction should just put more of themselves into it. It doesn't mean they have to write about corn pollen and eagle feathers. I get tired of that, too. People expecting that, all this "Indian wisdom" and four directions stuff, you know. It doesn't need to be that. But I would certainly like to see their lives and their culture in their work, from their own perceptions and experiences, and not so far removed that it's unrecognizable as being written by an Indian. There are a million science fiction writers out there. But being an Indian science fiction writer, well, that's something new and exciting.

c: What kinds of opportunities do you see for native writers and avenues that might be opening up that weren't previously available?

a: You know, I'm not sure. I know there's limited room for native writers to be successful. There's usually only room at the top for one at a time. There will be one who sells all the copies, and the rest of us are at various levels on the ladder. Eventually someone will come along and knock the one off the top, and somebody else will be the million-seller Indian, because there is only room for one there right now. I was happy with getting my small press book of poems out, *The Business of Fancydancing*. I had no idea it would take off like it did. I didn't expect it to, but I certainly wanted it to—I dreamed about it, and I'm glad it did, but I would've been content to have a small-press career. That would've been fine. I think people have to be content and comfortable with the idea of that. I mean, we'd all love the huge audience, and we haven't had as many opportunities to get it as other writers, but you know as well as I do that we're going to go out of fashion. I was right in the middle of it, and it's going to start tailing off now, unless something takes off. There are all these Indian books out, most of them written by non-natives, but they're still classified as Indian books, and they're going to glut the market with these bad books that nobody buys. Then the publishers aren't going to want to publish Indian books anymore because they don't sell. And they don't sell because they're awful. The good writing will be ignored again, and it will have to go back to the small presses where good writing is always published the most. For ten or fifteen years it will go like that, and then we'll resurface again because some book will come out of the woodwork and sell a lot of copies. It's like the stock market—be patient—it always ends up about the same anyway.

c: You sound like you're becoming schooled in this publishing experience. That must be trying after a point, dealing with the trappings of big-business publishing.

a: It's definitely big business. I sit down and write it, and it's art. The second it leaves my house it becomes commerce. And it's commerce with artistic intentions, rather than what I write now, which is artistic with commercial intentions. Yeah, it's frightening. It's like, "What am I? A pet rock?" You get the feeling that everything about you, you're selling. As a writer, you're selling yourself. When I do these readings and I go on book tours, I'm selling myself, which is dangerous. Because that can get very seductive. I've had the opportunity to sell my soul almost every day of the last couple years to somebody or something.

c: How do you avoid that?

a: You hear these stories about successful people who become jerks. I think they were probably jerks to begin with, and [laughs] success just provided an opportunity to magnify it. I wasn't a jerk to begin with, and I'm not going to let this experience make me become a jerk. The best moments of all of this are not selling all the books, which is great. I like the money, and I love the traveling and a lot of the people I've met. But the best things about it are times like when we were walking in a mall in Spokane, and these tough little Indian boys with all these problems of their own came running up all excited to see me. Because I'm "Sherman, the Indian writer." Those are the moments that are most important. Or when I do young Indian writers' camps and workshops, the kids just flock and listen to you. And you walk from classroom to classroom, and they're stopping you in the halls to read their poems and stories to you. That's the best part of it. Knowing that if somebody like that had been around earlier, I might not have had to go through as many of the bad things that I did. Knowing that the native writers who are spending time with younger writers are getting one of them, two of them, ten of them, a hundred of them, whatever, to start writing. And it doesn't matter if they publish or ever have a book. It's that they keep writing and realize that their thoughts and their stories and their emotions are valid and valuable, and that's the most important thing we do.

LITEFOOT

A darkened gymnasium on a small reservation is filled with young people crowded before a stage flashing light and shrouded in fog. A bass beat reverberates. Out of the fog, a young man, tall and strong, steps into the spotlight, bringing a message of the realities of being young and Indian in America. "Are you proud to be Indian?" his deep voice challenges. And the gymnasium is transformed by the answering call echoing into the early autumn night. Young voices, raised together as one, unified and strong, responding with the power of hearts meeting spoken word, wearing the rhythm of rap.

Billed as the "first Native American rapper," Litefoot, a Cherokee in his twenties from Tulsa, Oklahoma, has been carrying a message to the young people about facing today's realities by understanding the past and empowering themselves to embrace the future.

After an RCA record executive offered him a "deal" on the condition that his lyrics not be "Indian . . . because Indians don't buy tapes—they buy alcohol," Litefoot walked out the door and started his own label, Red Vinyl Records. His albums "Seein' Red" and "Good Day to Die" have swept through Indian Country and received radio play throughout the country. He has traveled extensively nationally and internationally, receiving rave reviews. He has starring roles in the films *The Indian in the Cupboard*, for which he won the Best Actor award from First Americans in the Arts, and *The Song of Hiawatha*, for which he won Best Actor award from the American Indian Film Institute.

In this interview, conducted prior to the filming of his first motion picture, Litefoot speaks on rap, gangs, and the vision that motivates the work he has chosen.

E. K. CALDWELL: The original use of spoken word with music by a native performer started primarily with John Trudell. Has he had any influence on your work?

LITEFOOT: With rap, I listened to more mainstream rap groups like Run DMC, Sugar Hill Gang, and Public Enemy. That's who really influenced me with rap. I didn't start getting hip to John Trudell's work until later on. I haven't had the opportunity to meet him, although I would like to do that sometime.

C: Are you performing mostly to native audiences or also in mainstream venues?

L: Basically, I found that if I was going to be the first Native American rapper that, by putting "Native American" before "rap artist," I had an obligation to the People first. I've centered myself on this tour, and in everything I do, even with the lyrics to the music, on our people. Once our people get it, and I feel comfortable that I've made that 110 percent effort to reach them, then maybe I'll worry about getting out there in the mainstream music market. But it's not in my plans for the future. I really don't care if the mainstream industry buys any of my tapes, because that's not what I'm here for. I'm here for our people. And I'm hoping through Red Vinyl Records to be able to provide opportunities for other young native rap artists. It's about helping each other.

C: How long have you been involved?

L: 1995 will be my eighth year. I've been with different groups, and I've been in the studio learning everything I could. The past two and a half years I've spent performing. This is the end result of all the effort that went into the years before.

C: You speak strongly about young Indian people not becoming involved in gangs. Many people say that gangs aren't really "our" problem, that it's an urban problem. Are you seeing gangs spread throughout the reservations?

L: I think that when people say this isn't a problem on reservations and with our youth, that it's an excuse not to do anything about it and for them to stay in their comfort zone. It's everywhere, and we need to wake up and deal with it and not pretend it isn't happening. Now's the time to deal with it and not wait until it gets worse. Now is the time to show the little ones that this gang mentality is ignorant. Have someone stand up and show them and say, "Look at them punks. They ain't about nothing. They won't stand up for nothing, really. And when you want to stand up to them, stand up to them, and they'll have to run away from you, because they ain't about jack. Because you're strong, and they're weak, and they don't know what to do with people who stand up to them."

C: There's been talk that you have received threats from gangs.

L: When I was little my dad told me that whatever you do, if you're not rippling the waves, that then you're not doing anything. So whenever I do something that I believe in and feel strongly about, [*laughs*] then I'm throwing boulders in the water. There were some people telling me I'm not very well liked in the gang community, and that there's possibly going to be some people who will make trouble because of things I say. If it's my time to go, and I go for speaking the things that I believe in and the things the Creator gave me to speak on, well, then that's my path to go then. I'm not afraid. The more the Creator brings things my way, and the more I get out there and increase my visibility, then more people are not going to like the things I'm saying, and they will want me to shut up. And I'm not going to shut up.

C: What do you think the gang mentality is really about?

L: I think that because in our communities, in a lot of senses, there's no real strong traditional cultural things to cling to. We're not getting taught those traditional things. There's not a lot of high self-esteem. So, when they [the youth] get out there in those cities and they see the African-American cultures, they look strong and like they have pride, and they got their own thing. Or like in the Latino communities with these *vatos* and all this talk about Latino pride. These kids look at this and say, "Look at what they got going on with their people and then look at back home. I'm going to go and be down with that, because that's better than back home." But you can look at it like you can be some of the founders of our own thing, of reestablishing our pride and our self-esteem, and getting our things back. That's what I want them to look at—the fact that no matter what color they claim, they're always going to be Indian, because that's what they were born, and that's their "gang," not in the other communities where they are being drawn to find some identity.

When I look at the people out there that they're taking bullets for because they're in the wrong place at the wrong time, well, I wouldn't go get shot at for none of them punks, [*emphatically*] none of them. Because they don't care about me. They don't have my best interest at heart. Even if they did care about me, what is it that I'm going to die for? When I go to my grave, what will I leave behind as why I died? I would've followed Crazy Horse and done whatever he wanted. Or Geronimo. I would have followed those men. Because they were about the People. Maybe if I would have been back in the day, I would've led some people. But I sure wouldn't stand for two seconds with these other punks, because, to me, they're weak. They're followers. And they don't know what they're being led into, and that's weak. It's not in our people to be followers like that.

c: Do you think part of the identity the young people are looking for in this mentality of violence has to do with looking for a family that is based in some kind of strength they can actually see? And having a place to belong?

l: Yeah, I would say that. They think they can get this feeling that there is somebody I can count on there. It's a false sense of hope and be-longing, a facade. People want to think it's there, but we have to real-ize that it's not there. When it comes right down to the wire, people don't have each other's backs like they say. Drugs and all that goes with that—using, selling, whatever—it turns out to be a very selfish way of life. Because it's all about money. And money gets people greedy. That whole thing out there is not what it seems to be. People that are really in it and are not the wannabes, well, they don't want to be in it. If they had another alternative solution to getting out of it, providing themselves a lifestyle that they could be comfortable in, well, they would take that in a second. It's not fun to be walking around out there wondering if you're going to get shot everyday, or to have to wonder if you're going to go to jail or end up in prison for twenty-five years. It's not fun to have that kind of pressure at fifteen years old or fourteen or thirteen.

c: Do you think the youth respond better to hearing the message in this rap format?

L: The music goes in and opens the door, and the message just goes right in. I'm not talking at them. I'm talking with them. I know it touches them because they come up and tell me at the end of the show. And they don't have to do that—it's not required. They do it because it's touched them, and I know that some of them are starting to see things a little bit differently.

c: You are on the road constantly and have a lot of exposure to people, many of whom are looking to you for all kinds of answers and attention. How do you deal with the stress of that? Especially with the young women whose hearts beat faster just looking at you. [*Laughs*] And probably some of the older women, too, from the comments I overheard at your performance.

L: I would say that I know what I'm supposed to do. I know I have to watch what I do. For one thing, I can't be out there talking about respect and then be having sex with basically every girl who screams at concerts or comes on to me like that. Sometimes it wouldn't be that hard to pursue those things, but that's not what I'm out there for. I am old enough to realize in a very realistic sense that if I do get with that girl, I am going to be gone the next day, and I've done more damage to her than I ever thought about doing good for her. That's what I'm going to leave her with and that's negative. I would rather leave her with something that the Creator has given to me to give to her rather than something physical or something that is going to be fleeting and just for a night. I know that she might think that's what she wants, but it's not really, in the long run. She should seek some-body who will show her respect, and *be there for her*, and support her taking care of herself and being strong. That's what I want to leave her with.

The way I deal with people pulling on me all the time—well, I al-ways said that no matter whether there was one or a thousand and one people standing in line for autographs, I would sign every one. I have a responsibility to those kids. I might only be there for a few sec-onds, and I want to do everything that I can while I'm there. I always want to remember that. There's been times that I've been signing au-tographs, and I'll be yawning. I don't want them to think I'm bored with being there, or with them, but I may not have had sleep for the past two days. It's becoming harder as far as fan mail because it's stacking up, and I can't get to all of it as fast as I want to. (You might want to put this in there so those people who have written me will know.) I don't really have five seconds to sit down and respond to it right now. I write all the cards myself. It's one small way of saying thank you for your support and for being there for me. It's so cheesy to have someone type up a letter and then you sign it and Xerox thousands of them. I mean, who wants that? I wouldn't want it, if it was me. The least I can do is try to write back, but it's becoming harder and harder.

c: What motivates you to keep going?

l: I want things done about child abuse, about drugs. I want things done about men not respecting women. About women not respect-ing themselves. Broken families. Gangs. To have people see these things and then be willing to come forward and make a stand and say, "I'm willing to do something about it."

I see too many youth organizations now that don't even know what the hell they are there for, and they're just a big social gathering ev-ery year. And that's just not what I'm about. They got millions of dol-lars and don't do nothing. What's wrong? Where is that money going? They need to bring a couple of strong young people from every reservation, the ones who want to make change, and intensively work them—not just about our things, but to show them how to walk in both worlds. Show them how to be business people and how to motivate other people and how to speak and be productive, so that when they go back to the reservations they are strong and armed with knowledge. Then the weak ones will have someone to look to so they can learn to be strong. Bring people in and have different perspectives shown from the white world, because we have to walk in that world and know how to make it in that world. We're not going to do it if we don't ever get the education. And then, after this exposure, to go at night and sweat and show them we have to do both. If we don't learn how to do both, we're history. We've already been written off as being history. And it's time for us to come back, and not just come back, but come back hard. Come back and make the people who died so we can be here proud of us. That's what motivates me.

c: Would you like to talk about the movie role for *Indian in the Cupboard* you recently accepted?

l: Now the Creator is opening up the next level. I don't know how I got this movie. I didn't call them up and ask to try out. They called us. There are actors out there that have been struggling for years to get a part. I'm even feeling bad because I'm thinking about all those people who are just wanting more than anything to be actors and trying to bust their butt to get into the movie industry, and here I am, doing it. When I got the phone call that says, "Yeah, they want you," I went out and I prayed. Because I wanted to acknowledge to the Creator that I knew it came from Him, and that's why I got it. It's almost like a promotion. [*Laughs*] Really, though, it's like I've taken what He's given me and done everything I could do with it, and now He said, "Good. Now go to the next level and increase the audience for when you go back out there again."

c: What is *Indian in the Cupboard* about?

l: It's based on a children's book. This little boy gets this toy Indian, and he puts it in this cupboard to keep it safe. The next morning he hears

pounding in that cupboard, and he opens it, and that Indian has become alive. The Indian doesn't know what to think because he's On-
ondaga, and he got pulled out of 1761. It's kind of like Quantum
Leap. He had his own life going on, and now he's in this cupboard. So
he and the little boy get acquainted. He knows how to speak English
because he's been fighting with the British against the French. They
develop a relationship and learn about each other. Then the boy gets
curious about what other things can happen in this cupboard, and he
starts putting other toys in there, like GI Joe and Spider Man and the
Ninja Turtles, and some big fights break out. It's really going to be a
big kids' movie.

C: Who is producing and directing it?

L: The people who did *E.T.* Frank Oz is going to be the director. He's di-
rected *Little Shop of Horrors* and *Dirty Rotten Scoundrels*, and he was
also the voice of Yoda in *Star Wars* and Big Bird on *Sesame Street*. So
he's reputable, and he's really a nice guy. He's also concerned that we
don't feed into stereotypes with this character. He wants him to be a
real person. None of that "Me want go eat food" and all that. He already talked to Oren Lyons about some of the things involved in the
movie. I want to get with Oren Lyons as far as how I present my character, clothing-wise and character-wise. Everything I've done with
my work has been to destroy stereotypes about our people, and I
don't want to do anything to promote destructive images. The stereotypes that it breaks down in the movie will go right along with
what I've been doing out here.

C: Lately in many of the interviews I've been doing, one of the topics
that comes up repeatedly is the controversy going on about blood
quantum. Would you like to comment?

L: I think blood quantum is a white way of thinking, a government way
of thinking. It's ignorant. Look at other races who are strong, like the
black people who have come so far in their struggle. They don't be
running around saying "halfbreed" and all that. They don't go into
the United Negro College Fund and say, "Well, I have to show you my

card because I'm only half black." And what do our people do? Well, they say to one another, "You're not Indian enough!" Well, what the hell is Indian enough? You know, back in the day, did we have cards amongst our own people? When a brother would come from somewhere else, like the Lakota visiting the Cheyenne, did they check everybody at camp for their cards? Did they say, "Look at this baby. It's too light." Maybe someone had sex with a soldier, or maybe someone white had been adopted into an Indian family. Once he had proved himself in terms of the principles the people lived by, he was in there. He had completed what was required of him. He was accepted. Period. Like, look at Crazy Horse. He was short, and his hair was brown and curly. He had grey eyes. Now tell me that's your stereotypical Indian. He was littler than everybody else. Now, lots of people would like to think that Crazy Horse was this big tall Indian. He wasn't dark skinned. Hell, if people saw Crazy Horse today, they'd be saying, "Look at that halfbreed!" Or they'd say, [*laughing*] "He must be one of them Cherokees! He—ey."

I think that this blood quantum thing is just another way the government has successfully brainwashed people. You can't look at it as anything other than propaganda. They've thrown this out there to our people, and we've taken it and said, "Ok, this is one more way that you can scatter us and divide us." You know, divide and conquer, that's their whole thing.

When black people were forcibly brought here, the white man said, "You don't have any name anymore. No religion. No tribal identity." Just look at where those folks have gone in the short time they have been here, and not by being Zulu or Swahili or whatever, but by being black. Look at us and how long we've been here—longer than anybody. And where are we at? It's like, "Well, I'm Choctaw, or I'm Chippewa, or I'm Paiute or whatever, and my tribe is the only thing." Well, so what? We are all related as Red People. We are one people. Keep your traditions and your ways that are specific to your tribe, but realize that if we are ever going to get anywhere, that if we are ever going to come up, you've got to put that ignorant narrow thinking out of your way and come home. Take the principles of traditions and apply them in the contemporary world. It's not impossible to do that. It's very possible, but we have to stop fighting among ourselves.

Look at Malcolm X and Martin Luther King and their leadership. How many cities have I been to where I have seen MLK Boulevard and this street and that street. And Martin Luther King Day as a national holiday. Do we have Sitting Bull Day? Do we have Geronimo Day? No, what we have is people taking the Paha Sapa, the sacred lands of the Sioux, and they slap four presidents on there and say, "Thank you, we respect you." Yeah, right. They take our people and make football teams out of them. Who do we blame? Ourselves, that's who. We are the ones who let it go that far. We cannot allow ourselves to be reduced to comic book characters and cartoons. How can we expect ourselves to be taken seriously in today's world? We can't wait twenty years. We can't wait fifty years. We've got to come back, and we've got to come back now! We've got to do everything we can to give children who aren't even born, and children who are young right now, a head start. They don't deserve to grow up and see Injun Joe get pushed off the mountain by Bugs Bunny or that tomahawk crap. It's time not just for our people to get a wake-up call, but for America to get a wake-up call. Before I'm even concerned about jacking with the rest of America, we've got our own problems to work out, and [we've got to] quit this ignorant thinking. Wake up. See what's really going on. And get off your butt and do something about it.

C: You speak about your generation being the seventh generation and the responsibility they need to take on, how they have to go out and find out what they want to know instead of waiting for someone to bring it to them. What kinds of responsibilities do you see the young people taking on now?

L: There's a girl at Rosebud, Emily Whitehat. She went alone to a shareholders meeting where they were selling all the land. She stood up in a tribal council meeting and said, "You say you're going to do this and that for the youth, but look at what you're doing. We're the people who are going to be stuck with what you're doing here today, and you're not doing any of this for us. You're in here for yourselves. And you don't care. You don't even think about the future." And she said, "I'm sick of being weak and not saying anything. And I'm going to say things when I want to say them." And so the head of their tribe made her his assistant.

c: You think the youth have the kind of power to make the adults listen and make changes?

l: I know they do. In Arizona there was a tribal council member who said that when he was a boy they were told not to say anything, that their time would come. And that's a lot of the mentality our kids have today. We don't have time to wait now. We can't be sitting around for ten or fifteen years and do nothing when there's a whole useful, talented group of young people out there. We need them now. We walk in both worlds today. Today is different than yesterday, and we have to adapt. We have to fight today differently than we did back in the day. We have to use our minds differently. We have to be educated. We have to learn the white man's game and be better at it than he is— so we can beat him at it. That's how we're going to get things done for our people. By venturing out and going off the reservation and having our voices start being heard all over this country. By starting little fires burning all over, and once we get those fires going, coming back to the rez and helping people. Help the ones coming up so they can go and keep that fire burning. This generation is the one that's going to probably make that older generation feel bad and be saying, "Look at what these young people are doing, and what have we been doing?" A woman told me that she went to the sweat lodge for the first time in her life, and her daughter took her. Her daughter knew the ways, and she was telling her mom what to do with the sage and whatever. The woman said she just got chills, and she started crying in there. She felt like she had let her daughter down, and that she should have been the one to tell her daughter about these things. She felt like she'd been robbed of the experience of the joy of teaching her children their ways. That's just one example of what's going to come about from this generation. We have all of the makings of getting huge things accomplished. Maybe my whole thing in this life is just to spark that. And I have done the best I can to generate that spark.

JESSE HUMMINGBIRD

Storyteller. The word conjures an image of words and intonations, rising and falling, listeners opening ears and hearts when the story is well told. Traditionally it is also visual, the gestures and facial expressions adding dimension, helping to bring the story to life. How often do we remember the visual artist as storyteller?

Cherokee artist Jesse Hummingbird loves a good story, especially the old stories of the People. An award-winning contemporary artist, he bases his work on these stories and traditions, teaching people to listen with their eyes.

Born in 1952 in Tahlequah, Oklahoma, and raised in South Carolina, Hummingbird received most of his classical training at the American Academy of Art in Chicago. He established himself as a successful printer, graphic artist, and commercial illustrator. But he wasn't telling the stories closest to his heart.

More than a decade ago he began creating work that expressed his understanding of traditional stories and themes. He paints in the traditional "flat" style of earlier native artists, using shadowless subjects with inlining. Using the same palette in all his work, he mixes his own paint for each layer, emphasizing intricate detail and bold colors.

His work has been well received and is shown throughout galleries in the United States. Concern for young artists prompted his decision to donate a portion of all sales to a native artist scholarship fund.

Hummingbird sees no conflict in using a contemporary style to reflect tradition. "No matter how difficult, I want people to know I'm proud of my culture and traditions. I want to preserve what we have left as I create the new."

E. K. CALDWELL: What are the origins of the "traditional flat style" of painting?

JESSE HUMMINGBIRD: People that study Indian art refer to the "Kiowa Five" who went and studied with Dorothy Dunn in the late 1930s and early 40s in Santa Fe. They brought that flat style of the hard outline with an inner line and no dimension to Oklahoma and the Southern Plains. Cecil Dick came in the next wave. He used that same style, except the Cherokee guys, like him and Bill Rabbit, started doing the flat landscape behind their work instead of doing one person on a white background. My work itself is contemporary, but the overall idea is still from that Oklahoma traditional style.

C: Were there earlier Cherokee artists, like in the 1800s, that were known and recognized in the art world?

H: A few collectors saw the importance of it, and you will see some work in museums here and there. People didn't sign their work. It would be really unusual to find any Cherokee art that had more than initials on it.

A lot of the elders had trouble with the generation before me, and even my generation, because they think we are so egotistical about the name recognition thing. Unfortunately some of us are like that. Some want to be big names and be a "star." Signing work probably didn't really start until the 1950s, when people started wanting to know who the artist was.

C: Would you comment on the significance of the indigenous artists' role within the cultures they represent?

H: In the Cherokee culture the most "important" people are the leaders and the healers. An artist should only be there as an ambassador and nothing more. The personality should not overwhelm what the artist is doing in his culture. No painter should become more important than the leaders and healers of their tribe.

At the same time, we don't want to live in obscurity. We are contemporary people. I am happy working alone at home, but you also have to go and meet people and do shows. It's the hardest thing because we really do have a foot in both worlds. You can't be successful unless people know you, but traditionally ego shouldn't be the thing you concentrate on most. It's a fine line to walk and not always an easy one.

c: Many of the old traditional Cherokee designs are compared to Mayan work. What is your opinion?

h: My generation (I'm 43) and my friends Bill Glass Jr., Mike Daniel, and some other artists from Oklahoma drew a lot of our influences from the Mound Builders. We went from the Mound Builders to looking at the Mayan art. When I was going to night school I read an article in a 1940s *National Geographic* that said the Cherokees were originally from at least as far south as the Amazon Basin and that influenced the craftspeople. I don't really know what all is true and what isn't, but it has influenced us young guys a lot in our work. [*Laughs*] But, who knows? We might have it all mixed up!

c: You paint a lot of masks and dancers with masks.

h: Cherokees did have ceremonial masks. Some of them were used in things like the booger dances. These dances could be described almost as theater. The last known depictions of the booger dance were done in a log cabin. The whole idea of the booger mask was that they would depict alien things, like the interaction with the white men. The human characters never show their hands—they are always cloaked in the blanket. Only the animals and the spirit characters were allowed to show their hands. The stories acted out could be humorous or sad, sometimes both.

We also had masks that were more "primitive" that we hung in our house for power and protection against illness and bad weather and to help if anyone was thinking bad thoughts about you—stuff like that. My little paperwork masks with the feathers and things are really just my contemporary version of that.

Just because these come from something in my tradition, people shouldn't be thinking they're all heavy and spiritual or something. They are artwork, plain and simple, because I am just an artist.

c: Are there symbols that you consciously avoid because they are considered sacred?

H: I have seen people who are doing depictions of things that are "too accurate" in terms of how you do medicine. It never occurs to me to even consider that. If I have a symbol in my work, it will be nothing more than a basket, a mat, or a shell quartz design that is probably well known and common amongst our people.

It would dangerous to use symbols in my artwork and pretend this was some sacred painting. It's been proven to me a long time ago those things are not to be used that way in artwork.

C: If you could envision the artistic legacy you will leave to the generations to come, what would it be?

H: People think I put a copyright symbol in front of my name because it is a "C" inside a circle. But it is there to tell my friend Cecil Dick, who's gone on, that he is remembered. His influence on me is not forgotten, and that symbol before my signature is to let him know that the circle hasn't been broken. If someday someone was to put a "J" with a circle around it on their work, that would be good enough for me.

C: What advice do you give to young artists?

H. The young people might think traditional things aren't important, but they still need to learn things.

I remember a man from when I was a boy, Mr. Vann, who made his own bows and arrows for the Cornstalk Shoot. His arrows never broke, and his bows were always true. (My brother told me later that he was the only one who knew those old chants for those bows.) I went there, and he had his work going. You could see his mouth moving. I thought, "Pretty neat. This reminds me I'm an Indian." Then I would just go on my way instead of going over and watching and learning about how he did what he did. I missed out on that.

It's important to hear those voices. They have to have enough of the old songs so that when it comes time for them to sing their songs that it's based on something from the old ways. Like rock 'n' roll started from the blues and jazz, you have to have enough background in the old ways to make your own songs mean something.

C: Would you comment on the pan-Indian art that seems to be flooding certain markets, much of which is done by non-native people? There seems to be conflict between cultural appropriation issues and the idea of artists' freedom of expression to create whatever they want to create.

H: In Western art, three-quarters of the work is Indians. I don't resent that, but somehow they [the non-Indian artists] get put into a "fine arts" category while the authentic Indian artist gets put into the "crafts" category, basically saying we're not "fine" artists. They seem to see our work as "quaint." I have a problem with that. Recognition in that "art world" helps us make a decent living. When one of these cowboy artists gets the recognition, the public seems to think it's more accurate than when an Indian artist does it.

I'm a board member of the Indian Arts and Crafts Association. This association lobbied and got laws passed in New Mexico and Arizona that help protect Indian arts and crafts. I got a letter from our executive director that informed me that the federal government is not going to get the funds for the Indian Art Board in Washington DC that was going to be the watchdog of the whole industry.

My biggest concern right now is all this fraudulent stuff going on, in jewelry especially. Look at these ads, like the Coldwater Creek catalog. There is a lot of Indian-looking jewelry in it, but only a small percentage is made by Indians. I have a Hopi friend who is involved in a lawsuit against a manufacturer who sent his work over to the Philippines and had it knocked off. They even kept his hallmark on it! You can't help but resent that. You have to take some kind of action.

People don't realize that whenever you buy a dreamcatcher that's made in some other country, you're basically hurting me as a painter. You're hurting anyone who makes authentic work, like the potter and the kachina maker and so on. People many times don't know that they're buying imported knock-offs. Anytime you buy imported goods you're affecting the last American handmade goods, and that

JAMES WELCH

Contemporary native literature and *James Welch*. The two are most times mentioned in the same breath, whether you are sitting in a university classroom or in an informal circle of native writers.

Nearly three decades ago, when native literature was a new idea to mainstream American publishers, James Welch, a mixed-blood Blackfeet/Gros Ventre, published a volume of poetry, *Riding the Earthboy 40* (World, 1971). Four years later, in 1975, he released his first novel, *Winter in the Blood* (G. K. Hall), which has been called "an influential classic in the birth of contemporary native writing." In the years since these two books appeared, Welch has become one of the country's most well known novelists, winning the 1986 *Los Angeles Times* Book Award for his historical novel *Fools Crow* (Viking). He has twice won the Pacific Northwest Booksellers Award. With these and his two other novels, *The Death of Jim Loney* (Harper and Row, 1979) and *The Indian Lawyer* (Norton, 1990), on international library shelves, in 1994 he released his first nonfiction work, *Killing Custer: The Battle of the Little Big Horn and the Fate of the Plains Indians* (Norton).

Killing Custer grew out of a documentary film project with award-winning filmmaker Paul Stekler, *The American Experience: Last Stand at Little Bighorn* (WGBH Educational Foundation, 1992). Following the documentary's airing on PBS, Welch expanded the story into book form. There are probably more books written about the Battle of the Little Big Horn than any other singular battle in the history of the United States. Welch surmises this is for one simple reason: "It's because the Indians won. If Custer had won that battle, it would be just a footnote in history." Welch's book is unlike any other written to date about that battle. Why? Because it is the only account that is told from the Indian perspective.

In a review written by Sherman Alexie (who wrote *The Lone Ranger and Tonto Fistfight in Heaven* and who is interviewed elsewhere in this collection), Alexie states: "He gives us all a look at a tragic time in American history, a sharper examination of what those tragedies have taught us and what we have all failed to learn. Above all, Welch confirms and mourns the fact that the war between Indians and whites has never ended. It may be the first history book written for Indians. I'm one Indian man who listens to this book and gives it an honored place in my home."

James Welch has given us more to consider. As he returns to writing novels, we can all look forward to more good reading and learning from this soft-spoken, astute, and deeply intelligent author.

E. K. CALDWELL: Other writers have referred to you as one of the "trailblazers" of native literature. Do you feel like a trailblazer?

JAMES WELCH: I published my book of poems in 1970, and Scott Momaday had published *House Made of Dawn* a couple years before that. So I have been around a long time. As far as being a trailblazer, there were people starting to write at the time I was writing, and it's just kind of mushroomed. I had some success, and my books have been taught in courses and so on, so I've been awfully lucky.

C: How do you see, from the time that you started writing, the evolution of contemporary native literature?

W: Well, I think it's been evolving very naturally. A lot of the early books, novels, short stories, and some of the poems have been pretty narrative. They reflected an Indian way of looking at the world and of telling stories. Today the same thing is mostly true. People are writing about their own experiences or experiences of their particular tribe, their reservations, or urban situations. It's a very natural way that it's evolved. So far most of the settings have been reservations, small towns, or whatever. I think it will evolve next to more about urban Indians.

C: In the past two and a half decades, how have you seen the perceptions change about who we are as Indian writers?

w: I'm not quite sure. One of the things that I've noticed about Indian writers, almost from the beginning, is that they were kind of on the edges of their cultures, not traditionalists nor right in the center of things. Most of the early writers were like that, and many of the most well known Indian authors today were that kind of people. Now some of the writers like Simon Ortiz and Ray Young Bear and people like that are in the centers of their cultures. I'm hoping that more and more traditional Indians will be writing books.

c: What do you think has prevented people who are traditional from involving themselves in writing?

w: I have thought about this, and the only thing I can think of is that they are so involved with their own tribal culture and dealing with the world from that perspective, and it's time-consuming. Maybe they haven't had the time or taken the time to learn the new forms like novels, short stories, lyric poetry, and all that. A lot of people on the fringes of the culture had more college opportunities with writing courses and following the path of mainstream writers.

c: There are Indian writers who object to the idea of Indians writing in an autobiographical format, saying it is not traditional and is not tribal. Would you please comment?

w: Indian people have always been tribally oriented, and individuals don't focus always on themselves if they are to be part of the tribe. I know mostly about the Northern Plains tribes, and individual Indians would try to make their mark, and then they would be kind of brought down. The autobiographical thing with the emphasis on the "I" probably is foreign to tribal people. On the other hand, we live in a changing world, and I just don't see how Indian writers can ignore those kinds of forms. I think it's very interesting for people to tell their individual stories of how they were brought up, how they fit into both worlds, and how they live their lives in both the hardships and the triumphs. The autobiographical form is a valid one for Indian writers, simply because of the way it works. The books are published with mainstream publishers, and they're going to be read by mainstream people and not just tribal people. I think Indian writers might be shorting themselves not to use that particular form.

c: Might part of the reaction also be that there are quite a few self-identified "Indians" who are writing supposed autobiographies that range from self-important exaggeration to outright spiritual lies?

w: Yeah, I think that's the danger. A lot of people think or feel they identify with the Indian, and they really "wannabe" Indians. They write these autobiographical stories that are usually just badly written fiction. That's all the more reason for us to write our own stories—not just tribal stories but individual stories. There are these commercial publishers who just want to make money and publish these so-called spiritual books and so on, and it's shameful that this kind of thing happens.

c: Some say that everything we write is autobiographical. Do you think that's true?

w: I don't think so. Young writers do have a tendency to be autobiographical, especially in poems and their first stories. Eventually you reach a dead end when you do that too long. Then you have to reach out and tell other stories, much the way a storyteller does—he doesn't say, "I did this, and this happened to me," and so on. Just like traditional storytellers, Indian writers have to tell stories and make new stories.

c: In this time of "Indian fashionability," how can Indian writers avoid the seduction of becoming commodities?

w: You have to concentrate on your own work and not worry about publishing it until quite some time into your career. If you're going to sit down and write a novel, don't worry about how it will be received or perceived, either by the outside world or by your own tribal group. Do your research. Concentrate on the novel and write it. Then I think things will happen. In most of the publishing houses there are some good editors who really want authentic work written by Indians. Work that would really reflect the Indian worlds.

c: Would you comment on establishing a balance between the art of writing and making a living as a writer?

w: I've been writing for twenty-five years, and for the first half of my career I certainly didn't make enough money to live. I was fortunate that my wife is a teacher, and she didn't mind paying the bills while I was writing and trying to get established. It worked out very well for me, and I'm just so grateful to her. It's very difficult to make a living, not just for Indian writers but for any writers. Young writers just have to live as cheaply as you can and hope eventually someone will recognize the value of your work. It will come. You have to be ready and able to suffer all those things that go along with being a writer, especially early on. There is an audience out there. However, you have to be willing to stick with it and work harder than you ever worked.

Things are a lot better now than they were ten or fifteen years ago. People are wanting to know what Indians think. There is a lot more opportunity for that young writer to come out with a book that gets the front page of the *New York Times Book Review*.

c: It seems that much of the work being published is poetry and short stories. The novel doesn't seem to be a form that many Indian writers are really accessing.

w: Not for very long and not many yet. The ones who are doing it seem to have success. As soon as they [novels] come out, they get reviewed all over the place, and as far as I know, they seem to sell pretty well. I think the novel is the last form the Indian people will really get comfortable in. They say that there's an "Indian Renaissance" going on from, say, 1970 up to the present. I don't see any sign of its slowing down. I think it's even escalating, so this is a good time for Indian writers to be working.

c: There will be people who will read *Killing Custer* and accuse it of being "revisionist history." In looking at the word *revision*, well, what's so bad about that?

w: *Revisionism* usually gets a really negative connotation, especially among academic people. They have grown up with their own traditional histories and literatures. When a group of people come along, and they don't fall in line and do things the way they are expected to, and they write about the same incidents from a different perspective, well, this really bothers them [the academic people]. Then they call it "revisionist history" and give it a negative connotation, mainly because it may contradict their view of what's supposed to be "real." Especially in academia, and maybe even with the reviewers who are up there on their high horses. Revisionist history has to happen. Revisionist literature has to happen. So far we've only had this one perspective. It's like the Little Big Horn. History will say that nobody survived the Battle of the Little Bighorn. But we know that thousands of Indians survived it. We need their stories as survivors. These historians have only presented the white perspective.

c: When you're going after this other perspective, who is it, or is there anyone, you try to satisfy in terms of authenticity?

w: I guess you have to make your own best judgment. First you have to read and acquire knowledge about the various perspectives. Then you make your own judgments about what really happened. I think the viewpoint of an untrained historian like myself, after having absorbed the literature and so on, is as valid as that of the trained dominant traditional historian. People don't realize this, that their own perspectives are quite valid. We should be pursuing that more.

c: People who wrote historical accounts, well, they were just writers putting down their perspective. Sometimes it seems like historians see themselves as beyond question.

w: They're all products of their own culture. When they write their histories, it's assumed it is objective, but it's not. It's a product of their culture, and their culture is the dominant culture, and that's not the only perspective.

c: What kind of impact do you think this has on indigenous people's identity?

w: I know from my own experience that the Indians were portrayed as the "bad guys," and they were "massacring" white people. If you read those histories and take them at their face value, you can't help but think we must have been really bad people. This is why it is so important to have history presented from another perspective, so that Indian kids can read this history and see that we were fighting to defend our country and our loved ones. The invaders were encroaching on our country and were taking it away from us. So we fought. And they can feel proud that we didn't just cave in.

c: In the front of *Killing Custer*, there is a chronology of events, and one of the things listed was the discovery of gold in 1874, when the country was in a major economic depression. Then, in 1877, when Congress ratified the theft of the Black Hills, the economy took an upswing from the gold rush and the mining companies. Do you see parallels today in terms of that experience?

w: I think the government and industry consistently try to exploit Indians. They're out to make a buck, and I think they see reservations and Indian people as an opportunity. They're very smart about how they make it seem to the Indians that it is to their benefit to accept things like nuclear waste dumps. Or to mine all the minerals off Indian Country because once the minerals are gone, the land probably won't be reclaimed, and the Indians will be left holding the bag. They're still exploiting Indian people, but now they try to make it seem like a partnership. It's not a partnership. The long-term impact will hurt us.

c: How did you like writing your first nonfiction book?

w: I enjoyed it. I had never done anything like that so I was really nervous, a real amateur, learning by doing, but that was part of the fun. I don't think I'll do it again. [*Laughs*] I'm going back to novels.

c: [*Laughs*] Where you can just make things up?

w: Yes, I'm very comfortable doing that. [*Laughs*]

c: Has there been opportunity to do dramatizations of your novels?

w: There have been a lot of options taken out on my novels, but they haven't actually gotten around to making the movies. Since all of my main characters are Indians, they said they couldn't raise millions of dollars based upon Indian characters. There might be parallel characters where there is an Indian and a white guy, and that the white guy will be box office. They seem less willing to chance it with the Indian character being the lead.

c: Do you have any words for the young people who are having dreams about being writers?

w: I think people should write. Kids, and even older people, should write and should consider it a form they can do and feel comfortable in. I had a writing teacher who once said that writing poetry is an act of self-discovery. You find out a lot about yourself and your place in the world. I think any kind of writing is the same way. Even the physical act of writing makes you use your imagination and your intellect. We're not used to using our imagination. We all need that. It's a good thing. I encourage all people to write and at least give themselves the opportunity to have that experience.

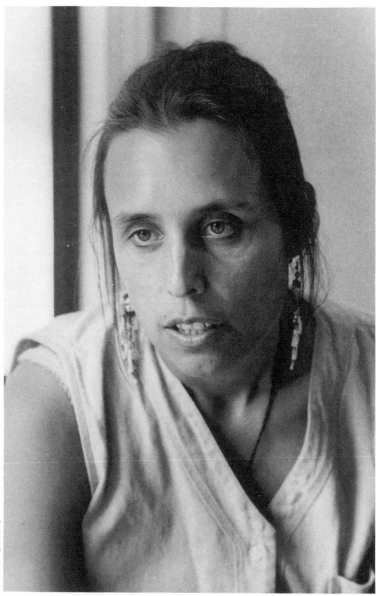

WINONA LADUKE

Winona LaDuke first gave expert testimony at a 1977 U.N. Conference in Geneva, Switzerland, regarding the exploitation of natural resources of indigenous peoples of North America and the impact of that exploitation. She was eighteen years old.

Already a student at Harvard, LaDuke stated she became "politicized" by a talk given there by Jimmy Durham when the International Indian Treaty Council (IITC) was establishing itself as the first Indian nongovernmental organization (NGO) to bring issues to the United Nations. In 1979, LaDuke prepared expert testimony for IITC that revealed the violations caused to indigenous populations by the exploitation of natural resources within their territories.

These testimonies marked the beginning of her lifetime commitment to the People. Her intense energy and keen mind have made major contributions in Indian Country, from local communities to the international arena, and have resulted in her international recognition as a speaker, writer, researcher, and tireless worker.

She has published extensively on issues of native economic development, environmental issues, and legal issues related to native affairs. Her legal research helped prepare litigation in many well-known cases, such as coal and uranium mining in the Southwest and title claims on the White Earth Reservation in Minnesota that resulted in challenging the constitutionality of the White Earth Land Settlement Act. She was also instrumental in stopping the huge James Bay hydroelectric project, which threatened four major rivers in Quebec and the homelands of the Cree and Inuit peoples living along them. A special report in *Time* magazine (December 1994) named LaDuke as one of "50 of America's most promising leaders under age 40."

Winona LaDuke has been gifted with a unique sense of vision regarding the survival of indigenous peoples. Her Anishinabe father (Vincent LaDuke) and her Jewish mother (Betty Bernstein LaDuke) have united in her blood the common histories of two peoples targeted for oppression and genocide.

Born in 1959 in East Los Angeles and enrolled at White Earth according to her father's traditions, LaDuke grew up first with both parents in the urban Indian community and then in Ashland, Oregon, with her mother, a well-known artist, who encouraged Winona to continue to embrace her indigenous heritage. A part of her was always drawn to go "home" to White Earth.

After graduating from Harvard in 1982, LaDuke accepted a one-year position as executive director of the Circle of Life High School on the White Earth Reservation. Her skill as an organizer led to her subsequent involvement in the development of Anishinabe Akeeng (1983–88), a community-based land rights organization. In 1989 she became the campaign director of the White Earth Land Recovery Project (WELRP), a land acquisitions and self-sufficiency project that she continues to oversee. The seed money for WELRP came from a Human Rights Award for twenty thousand dollars that LaDuke received from Reebok.

In 1985 she founded the Indigenous Women's Network (IWN), a continental network of grassroots indigenous women organizers and community workers, and continues as cochair of the organization. IWN publishes *Indigenous Woman* magazine, a biannual journal of native women's issues.

In 1995 IWN joined forces with the Seventh Generation Fund, a native foundation that supports grassroots indigenous initiatives in environmental justice and community restoration and that had named LaDuke its environmental program director in 1994. Together, the organizations launched "Honor the Earth, 1995," a tour of twenty-seven cities that included visits to young people on six reservations and that featured the Epic Recording artists Indigo Girls as headliners. The tour raised two hundred thousand dollars for indigenous environmental and community groups and was repeated in 1997.

In September 1995, LaDuke traveled to Beijing, China, where she was a plenary speaker at the United Nations Conference on Women. She also holds the position of steering committee representative of the International Council of Indigenous Women, which is seeking NGO status at the United Nations. LaDuke was the vice-presidential candidate on the Green Party ticket with Ralph Nader in the 1996 presidential election.

Currently Winona LaDuke lives on the White Earth Reservation with her children and animals when she is not on the road. It has been more than twenty years since that eighteen-year-old student first spoke to the United Nations in Switzerland, representing the concerns of this continent's indigenous people. Her ongoing contributions are many as she continues to demonstrate the power of persistence, politics, and prayer.

E. K. CALDWELL: With the current political shift in DC, there is renewed resistance to honoring indigenous rights combined with an environmental onslaught mentality. What suggestions do you have in terms of response?

WINONA LADUKE: I encourage people to be politically active, especially in their own community. My personal political belief is that you don't relinquish any right over yourself to termination by anyone in the corporate boardroom. That belongs in your community. You have to be really informed about what your tribal council is doing, and you have to directly participate in your own community. I don't believe the tribal council has the right to decide my destiny. That right belongs to our people. It's our elders who have the authority over us. I encourage people to think of that. In our experience on the 1995 Honor the Earth tour, all across the western area, sometimes the councils were present with the people and sometimes not, but the elders were always right there.

There are people everywhere who are struggling on these issues who sometimes win and sometimes don't, but they have the courage. That is the essence of what Honor the Earth is about, the courage and spirit of those people to struggle. At the closing show in Portland [June 1995] we honored four women: Janet McCloud, Margaret Flintknife Saluskin, Mililani Trask, and Myra Sohappy, who are exemplary in this struggle against the odds. We are the mothers of nations, and everything that is of concern to our nations is of concern to us. We have an absolute right to exercise that concern.

c: What primary environmental issues are people working on in indigenous communities?

l: The primary issue would be resource extraction. That's the overarching issue we have found. Whether that's mining or logging or whatever, it still comes down to resource extraction. A second issue is toxic dumping. For example, there has been a significant level of dumping in southern California. Another piece we're looking at is trying to protect communities who are just trying to have their way of life.

People need to become politically involved at this time and write to American congressional delegations to tell Congress what their position is on issues. Re-authorization of the Endangered Species Act is extremely important because its defeat can tear down a tool you can use. Anytime you have a tool like this, especially one that took the environmental movement twenty years to build up, you can't risk losing it.

In Alaska there is a horrendous level of taking from native people that is pushed by the Alaska congressional delegation. Two times now the indigenous people have defeated the opening up of the wildlife refuge. Now the Alaska congressional delegation put it on as a rider in the budget bill. They want to open up public lands and the Arctic National Wildlife Refuge to help reduce the federal deficit.

There is local sentiment there that is very anti-environmental. The Anchorage paper had a front-page story that said they wanted to call it the Arctic National Oil Reserve instead of the Arctic National Wildlife Reserve. How obscene. There's ongoing congressional action to decimate the region. To me, this situation in Alaska is just a microcosm of America, especially Indian Country.

c: Some say the healing that is going to come to our nations and to the planet herself is going to come first from the women. Do you believe that?

l: Yes. I've heard it said in a number of prophecies that this is the time of the women. I believe that both men and women have responsibility, but in my experience in grassroots community organizing, there are mostly women. There are reasons for that. For example, on my reservation the allowable number of fish for a woman or child is lower than for a man. I am on the front line of impact because I am a woman of childbearing age. So I have every right to be concerned. Women are mothers, and it is our responsibility to care for those things.

A lot of the colonialism that has occurred in our communities is reflected to us. On my reservation the entire tribal council is men. It is a male-dominated political structure of the Indian Reorganization Act government. Community-based organizations are often the only forum for women to exercise their rights and their responsibilities. That is not to say that we should be in every forum, but I know that I could not get a job on my reservation working for my tribal council. Many women are in the same situation.

We have the right to organize. We have the right to have a voice. A lot of those voices are not recognized by the BIA [Bureau of Indian Affairs]. And you know what? We don't need them! They tell us we can't do it, but like Mililani Trask says, "Just watch us."

c: If the grassroots work is getting done mostly by the women, how can we be more inclusive with the men and work together effectively?

l: Well, men need women and women need men. That is how we attend to our nations. We all have our roles. That is my belief and my practice. There are a lot of things that I cannot do, and there are a lot of things that they cannot do. It's not just physical strength that I'm talking about, but seeing the different sides of us. If the work is going to get done, we have to work collectively.

We desperately need recovery of traditional practice, because that's when the status of men and women is equal. In industrial colonial society, men and women don't have equal status. So these [our] men are told they have equal power and then are treated like shit. Then you get that pecking order syndrome that brings us all the way down. We have a lot of lateral oppression in communities between women and then between children. That is the impact of all that. There is so much recovery needed.

c: How can people address the lateral oppression that exists?

l: There are no easy solutions. Within our traditional beliefs there is a common factor of respect. Respect is the answer to lateral oppression. It is in the teachings to treat all that is around you and yourself with respect.

It is also analyzing exactly what is the problem. The problem is not usually just your spouse or your tribal council. The government created the tribal councils in their image. It was a total setup all along, and we end up blaming individuals. Individuals should definitely be held accountable for their unethical and criminal behavior, yet absent of context, you could end up with the same thing in another four years, unless you deal with the root cause of it. The sources of oppression itself.

c: We talk here about the need for political action in our communities. With the immediate survival needs being so urgent with many people, in everything from feeding and housing your kids to dealing with a wide range of abuse of chemicals and people, how do you convince people that political action can make a difference?

l: Unemployment, domestic violence, substance abuse—those and the many other problems that affect our communities are symptoms of a much larger problem which is based in unresolved historical grief. That we cannot control our destiny. We have our land and our language and our cultural practices stripped from us. I do not believe that you can heal a human without healing a community. You cannot heal a community without healing your land and your water. They are all so integrally related. There's plenty of work in all that for each of us.

My work is more in land and culture and environment, but I need people whose work is in other areas. I go to people who teach me culture because I am a student of our cultural practice, not a teacher. My view is that the only way to fix us is to fix all that. It is such a slow process.

If you look at this society, I do not believe you could be sane and not angry. It would be insane to look at this dominant society and accept what it is. If you think it's okay, then I think there's something wrong with you.

One of the things I've noticed, especially in areas like Alaska, is how people suffer from being prey to a predator. How can you recover when you stop one thing, and then they do something else to you! You fight off a clear-cutting, then they say they're going to put a dump on you. The Eyak people in the Cordova village are still dealing with the Exxon Valdez oil spill. Now [others are] going to try to clear-cut their entire area. Think about that. If you consistently threaten an animal's habitat, the animal goes insane. The animal stops having babies and becomes more and more frenetic. Watch wolves in captivity or animals in a zoo. They go insane. Then [people] wonder why our communities suffer as they do. It is a collective process. How can you live if every day when you wake up your first thought is that they are going to take away your primary source of life?

We have to recognize the big picture, and people need to support us. Non-Indian people need to recognize and support our right to live. We have that right to live and the right to ceremony, whether it is the ceremony to call back salmon or whatever our practice requires for the survival of our communities.

That's how you address that. I know I've gone kind of round-about, but that is my view. *Retraditionalization*. That's what they call it. Retraditionalization. Recovery of your own traditional practice. It is the foundation of healing.

c: The U.S. news coverage of the U.N. women's conference in Beijing portrayed a heavy-booted security mentality. What was your experience?

l: First of all, you have to recognize that China is not the United States. People have a different standard. It's a closed country that was overwhelmed by the presence of the largest U.N. conference ever. No third-world country has ever hosted a conference so large. The logistics were not perfect. I think people underestimated the impact of that many women and that many requirements on a country that's basically trying to feed a billion people.

The police were especially bad to the Tibetan women. They roughed them up and confiscated their materials and videotapes. I went to the U.N. committee with the Tibetan women to register a complaint after the third time they were accosted by Chinese authorities.

I did not notice that police were in my room, but my papers were in such disarray, I probably wouldn't have been able to tell anyway!

c: There was also a brief flurry in the media here about the comments Hillary Clinton made regarding women's rights as human rights. Any comment?

l: In my view, Hillary has some integrity and presented the issues well. We were pleased with her presentation. She was the co-convener of the U.S. delegation, and she probably even took the issues further than some of the people in the delegation might have. In terms of the context, we participated in both the nongovernmental organization (NGO) and the government conferences. At the NGO conference Hillary was considered conservative in the views presented. At the government conference she was considered more radical and outspoken. You have to look at that in terms of the continuum of political stature and standing.

c: What were the strongest things accomplished at the conference?

l: We got to present our issues in an international forum and be heard by a lot of women. There were about 115 women from around the world who presented a host of issues, ranging from trafficking of women, destruction of homelands, sterilization abuse, murders in police states, to cultural preservation issues. We got to broaden the context of what are women's issues and what are women's rights. The conference talked about women's rights as human rights. The rights of women, like the rights of indigenous people, are not within the purview of domestic nations. It's not just that nation's business but is an international human rights issue. We drew a lot of attention to things, and we got to hear a lot of stories that we would never hear otherwise.

We, as native women, forwarded some positions that stated that we did not support the mainstream women's movement position of gender equity. Instead we stated our support of women's rights to self-determination.

c: Please explain the difference.

l: In gender equity it pretty much says that women should be treated equal to men. I don't support that position, and the Indigenous Women's Network does not support that position. First of all, under international law, there is no precedent for gender equity. There is a precedent for peoples' rights to self-determination.

That means, for instance, in my cultural context, I do not want the role of a man. I want to have my own role as a woman. I want to have that valued and have the right to determine what role it is I want in my society. That is different than gender equity. It is a woman's right of self-determination. Our suggestion is that in an international context women are Peoples as indigenous people are Peoples. As such, we have rights to self-determination, and this better serves the collective interest of the world of women.

The second reason that we oppose the concept of gender equity is that largely what it does in the dominant society is to replace white men with white women in bastions of power. It does not deal with issues of race, class, and different "isms" in society or the fundamental construct of what the source of wealth is in the dominant society in relationship to indigenous people. Essentially living on stolen land and stolen resources. Women's right to self-determination addresses that. It says that I have a right to self-determination as much as an upper-class wealthy woman living in New York City, that my right to self-determination is equal to her right.

C: How do women who identify themselves as members of the feminist movement respond to this position?

L: I was an opening plenary speaker in Beijing and presented it there. We also talked about it throughout the conference. I heard broad acclaim for what we said, and I also heard some groans from some women whom I would classify as mainstream feminists.

I am in support of women, but the women's movement has not addressed issues of indigenous women. It has to be "reclaimed" by all of us who are women. It is not intended to be just the purview of upper-middle class white women, which is pretty much where it has been.

Therefore the primary issue that has been forwarded has been that of choice. I don't consider choice to be the primary issue of indigenous women. I think the basic issue of right to self-determination, whatever that might mean to the different groups of indigenous women, is the fundamental issue. This includes the right to determine control over your body, the right to be free from domestic violence, to be free from discrimination from whatever agency it is that discriminates against you, and the right to determine your future, regardless of what multinational corporation wants to take something from you. Those are fundamental rights and concerns of indigenous women, not the exclusive concern over choice. That is the major challenge we have for the women's movement itself.

c: Is White Earth the first reservation to launch a land recovery project?

l: No, other reservations have done it, but we're nonprofit, which means we are not affiliated with tribal council. This is good, especially considering that members of our tribal council got indicted recently, and it's about time! It's also a shame because they are trying to hide behind the cloak of tribal sovereignty. Their defense is a total misrepresentation of what tribal sovereignty is about. There is no denial that they committed these crimes. They are just saying that they are sovereign, and nobody can prosecute them. It's a total abuse of power.

c: Can the tribal court prosecute?

l: They appoint the tribal court judge. We have no power there. It has been a case of absence of civil rights here for years.

c: Does this upheaval present opportunities for women to become involved in the male-dominated tribal council?

l: I think it presents an opportunity for change. The chairman in the power structure has been there for about twenty years. People have run numerous times and have basically had elections stolen from them. This may be the first time, if we succeed in political work in the coming months, to actually have a fair election at White Earth. It is not necessarily just women who will change the tribal council. I think it is people who are truly concerned about their nation and who are traditionally oriented. Women are an essential part of that. It will take people who have some kind of vision when they look at tribal government and traditions.

c: Regarding land recovery issues, I have seen articles from mainstream papers that voice worry about tribes buying "private" land and increasing reservation holdings. Your comment?

l: My gut feeling is that they are afraid we will treat them as badly as their ancestors treated us. The reality is that is absolutely untrue. I come across it all the time. People say, "You guys are buying back all the land. You want all the land." And I say, "Well, a hundred years from now we're going to have at least half, maybe three-quarters of our reservation. Decisions are going to made by Indians. Privilege will not be maintained by non-Indians. We're going to live as equals." They are afraid of that because of all that has happened historically.

What is important to say about the White Earth Land Recovery Project [WELRP] is that we exhausted all our legal recourse, and we have had a tribal council who has not only had an absence of vision but who has been historically in collusion with the federal government. They could take a much stronger position, but they have not. As an individual tribal member, do I abdicate my responsibility and say, "Well, nobody's going to do anything, so I'm out of it," or do I say, "I have as much responsibility for my nation as my tribal chairman. I have as much right to determine my children's future as my tribal chairman does!"

That's what we're saying here at WELRP. We're saying that every Indian person has an equal responsibility to determine their future. So we're going to take on some of that responsibility here. We don't know if we have the right solutions because we are far from perfect, and we have nowhere near the amount of money to do what needs to be done, but we're going to get in there and we're going to continue working on it.

C: What do you think are the most successful aspects of WELRP?

L: We bought a thousand acres of land. We operate an organic raspberry farm and a maple sugar operation. We have an integrated Ojibwa language program and community development and environmental advocacy. We have demarcated our reservation borders for the first time in fifty years. We're working on a bilingual road sign project with the Department of Transportation. These things are representative of a range of our work. We are a multi-issue project that is founded on culture, land, language.

C: Is the financial aspect the most difficult?

L: Yes. We grew from a small project to a big project, and that has affected funding. Four-tenths of 1 percent of all foundation money in the country went to Indian projects when we started. Now seven-tenths of all foundation money in the country goes to Indian projects. Of that, 40 percent goes to non-Indians helping Indians. Of the remaining monies, about three-fourths of that goes to national organizations. So, you get somebody like us who went from being a "cute little environmental justice project" to a big project that is trying to serve the people, and we don't fit easily into their funding structure. The tendency of the funding community is to give seed money and walk away. Any farmer knows that you don't plant a seed and walk away. We are trying to diversify with direct mail marketing of our products and at the same time trying to leverage larger foundation multiyear grants. Our work is as legitimate as any national native organization. Someone needs to speak up for community work and community people and show that these struggles are bottom-line in the communities. Our future generations are at stake.

c: You have spoken about opportunities like the Honor the Earth tour to "politicize" the young people and ensure the future. Please explain.

L: When I was about seventeen and wet behind the ears, I was in school on the East Coast. Jimmy Durham came to talk at Harvard. He worked for the International Indian Treaty Council, which was the first Indian NGO that existed, and he was working on organizing the first nongovernmental U.N. conference. He said there was no such thing as an "Indian problem" and that what actually existed was a problem with the United States and Canada and Bolivia and Argentina. And that this was an international problem that we as indigenous people shared with the Palestinians and the people of South Africa and other peoples.

When that guy spoke, it changed my frame of thinking. I had been raised in American schools that always talked about the "Indian problem." Over the years, I had internalized the whole victim process, including blaming of the victim. I had not been able to look at reservations in an international context, in terms of the five hundred million indigenous people struggling to control their destiny outside of the U.N. nation-state framework. These nation-states are not recognized by the U.N. When he spoke, it was the beginning of the process of politicization because it changed the framework of my thinking from my own limited view. It took it [my thinking] outside to a broader analysis. "Politicization" is that process where consciousness expands into a broader context where you can think not only about what the problem is but what to do about it.

c: There are many people in our communities who openly state they are not political and do not want to be politically involved.

L: That in itself is political. Politics, well, I don't know what it really is. But what I do think is paramount is that we figure out a way to leave something for our children that is better than what we inherited. That process requires social change, and there are a lot of factors in that. It may be cultural. It may be ceremonial or working with your tribal council. It may be fighting a corporation. All of those have political aspects.

c: How do you take care of yourself?

L: I try to stay home as much as I can, and I have a good place with nice children and nice animals. It reaffirms for me what is life and what I am working for. I have a lot of conflicts in my own life, but for me, I heal through my work. It makes me feel better. Then I feel like my children are safe, and we can go get our berries or our maple syrup where we're supposed to, and that makes me feel better. When I'm on the road, many times I am in a place of reinforcing what I believe in, and I have the opportunity and the honor of being with people who are doing the same. That process restores you.

c: Do you have some words you would like to share specifically with the young women and men?

L: Believe in yourselves and your cultural foundations. Believe in the people that are your foundations. Learn the social history of your community's struggles. It will help you know who you are and where you come from. Recognize the value and the courage of so many people from so many generations, regardless of the color they are.

The reason we are here today is because someone struggled. It teaches you something about what you leave. Remember that quality of life is not equated with level of income. You can't buy happiness. Quality of life is equated with how you feel about yourself and how you feel about others. Whether you have clean air and water and whether you feel safe. Those are the things to understand.

DINO BUTLER

His ancestors were forcibly removed in the mid 1800s from their home-lands in the Rogue River area of southern Oregon and northern Califor-nia and marched to the Government Hill Agency on what is now the Siletz Reservation in Oregon. The impact of this forced relocation had a direct influence on his upbringing and the way he learned to make decisions about his identity as an indigenous man and his place in society.

Born April 8, 1942, in Portland, Oregon, and raised mostly in logging camps around Siletz, Darelle "Dino" Butler has walked a difficult path in his lifetime. He does not romanticize the steps of the journey and discour-ages young people from emulating his own youth and early adulthood.

At age thirteen, Butler was sent to MacLaren Boys School for curfew violations and "wandering" over one hundred miles from home. The anger that he carried within him further ignited there, and over the next two decades it fueled into a rage that threatened to become his only identity. Between 1956 and 1970, his continual arrests for assaults and related charges resulted in ongoing incarceration. The longest time he had outside of jails and prisons was six months.

In 1974 Butler was introduced to the American Indian Movement (AIM) and attended some of his first traditional ceremonies. Something within him shifted, and with this shift came the stirrings of a spiritual reawakening. His involvement with AIM took him to many native com-munities involved in the struggle against the U.S. government's ongo-ing disregard for indigenous rights and sovereignty.

On June 26, 1975, an FBI attack on the Oglala, South Dakota, spiri-tual camp resulted in the deaths of two FBI agents and one indigenous man. Butler was arrested and charged with two counts of murder. The 1976 trial, in which he and codefendant Bob Robideau were acquitted, drew national attention.

In the late 1970s Butler participated in the Minnesota Citizen's Review Committee on FBI misconduct, working toward the release of Leonard Peltier, who was convicted for the deaths of the two FBI agents. Butler's 1979 request for political asylum in Canada was denied because he returned to the United States to testify for the defense in Peltier's trial.

En route to a ceremony in Canada in 1981, Butler began an unexpected journey through the Canadian corrections system. He and his cousin, Gary Butler, were charged with attempting to murder two Canadian policemen. After the pipe was denied entrance into the courtroom, they refused to participate in the trial and presented no defense. They were found not guilty. The journey that he took through the jails and prisons there from 1981 to 1984 strengthened his spiritual resolve as he became actively involved in securing religious freedom and access to ceremonies for indigenous people incarcerated in Canada. These efforts resulted in the first indigenous ceremonies ever permitted in the Canadian corrections system.

This pivotal time in his journey brought a new awareness, showing him the devastating effects of the hatred that had taken root within him and those around him. It opened his heart to a new kind of healing and a commitment to respect all life.

In the past decade Dino Butler has continued on that healing journey. In 1992 he returned with his family to the Siletz area after living in the spiritual camp at Redwind in central California for nearly five years. He and his companion, Juanita Whitebear, and their family comprise part of the nucleus of the Oregon Native Youth Council, a grassroots organization that is dedicated to helping native youth and their families establish identity as indigenous people and that is not steeped in confusion and violence. His journey continues, relinquishing a legacy of hatred, embracing respect for all life.

Dino Butler's comments were collected during four interviews and are combined in this chapter.

E. K. CALDWELL: You wanted to make a statement about why you decided to do an interview.

DINO BUTLER: I would like to start with a story. I was taught that in the beginning Grandfather/Grandmother, the Creator, made this universe and created Mother Earth. Four families were put upon the earth to live in harmony and respect for life. The Black People. The White People. The Red People. And the Yellow People. He put each of these people in a different part of the world, and he gave them a way of life to live upon that land. He also gave them instructions about their way of life, and the instruction was that no one people would force their way of life upon another people. To me, if we tell this story right, all other things will become clear.

The reason I would like to do this interview is that I see a lot of what I consider to be confusion that is used to control our emotions and our actions. Instead of having the truth determine how we conduct ourselves in this universe, we let the confusion do that for us now. It's getting worse with each generation. It began for our people and our way of life when our ancestors were brought to the reservations as prisoners of war. I don't think we ever sat down as a people and as a nation to deal with what happened so it can be released and go on with our lives as a nation. Instead they just passed the bitterness and the confusion on to their children.

C: You said you would like to dedicate this interview to Anna Mae Pictou (Aquash).

B: Anna Mae was, and still is, an inspiration to me. Everything I do in my life, with my life, is dedicated to people like Anna Mae, who gave up everything she had to keep her beliefs alive. Her beliefs will always be alive as long as I'm alive in this world. My greatest desire is to be able to pass that spirit on to other people in the next generations so that we don't lose the reality of our existence. That's what always kept our people and all life alive and surviving in this world. To resist the things that separate the physical and spiritual beings. That's why I'd like to dedicate this to Anna Mae, who to me represents the spirit to all of our people.

C: How would you define the legacy of hatred?

B: It came with the Pilgrims because that's what they were running away

from. That confusion was brought from another land, and ever since they came here they have taught that.

When I grew up in this society, hate for anyone that was different than me was one of the strongest teachings that was taught to me. This was taught to me by my own family. The hate is a big mistake for us to be teaching our children. It is a tool that is used to oppress our spiritual beings. It's not a natural thing for us to hate. The hate of all life does not come from the Creator because Grandfather has not created anything that's meant to defeat us as human beings or to separate us. When we let the hate determine our actions, then we're denying our true identity that tells us to respect life.

We keep getting further and further away from our true identity, which is quite evident in the way that most of our people conduct themselves today. You look back over the generations, and our people knew their identity. They knew their relationship to the earth and all life. They respected all life. You didn't take life unless there was a real purpose. When they had to take life, they gave offerings to the spirit that life represented to them.

We can no longer base our struggle for liberation from a corrupt values system on hate for an enemy. Our struggle has to be based on something much stronger and more lasting. If we base it on hate, then all of our struggle is for nothing.

c: How has the legacy of hatred affected the American Indian Movement [AIM] in its evolution and where it is today?

b: When we started becoming acquainted with AIM and the teachings, a lot of us had come out of prisons, institutions, the orphanages, the bars, and years of being oppressed. We brought that hate with us into the movement. That's why we were so quick to pick up the guns to fight our enemy. Our enemy at that time was the government forces because they were the most visible ones who were causing pain upon our people and our way of life. I read this saying one time, "It's easy to die for a cause; it's a lot harder to live and work for that same cause." In the late 60s and early 70s, we were all willing to die for our beliefs—for our people. We didn't know what it was to live and to work for those same goals and to continue on.

I think that was the evolution that AIM brought to our people. To go from willingness to die for our people to willingness to live and to pass life on. The will to continue in this world. The will to resist, the will to live. To pass that on to the next generations and the next seven generations ahead of us.

c: Do you think that because people were young, both chronologically and spiritually, that this had a strong influence in AIM and caused confusion between people and how they treated one another?

b: We had all come from different aspects of this society that had no respect for us as human beings and as indigenous people. We carried a lot of resentments from all the bitterness, and that hate had control of us. AIM introduced me to spirituality that allowed me to identify to myself as an indigenous person of this land. I had no idea what it meant to be an indigenous person of this land. There was nothing that this society offered that allowed me to relate to myself as that. We were just learning how to walk as human beings.

c: You mentioned that with all these divisions within AIM that you think the movement has "stalled" spiritually. Would you explain that?

b: In the beginning of AIM, a lot of us brothers and sisters came together, and we formed a solid bond. We learned how to pick up that pipe, and we learned how to pray again and dance together and sing together. And we grew spiritually. We started fulfilling some of our responsibilities in this world through these teachings that we were learning. We progressed, and we became stronger, and we became more compassionate as people. One of our responsibilities in this world is to continuously learn within ourselves. We were working hard to do that in the beginning with AIM. We progressed to a point where we became Sun Dancers, pipe carriers, sweat lodge people.

Then we came to a point where I feel like we began to not learn any more. Because we do carry hate and refuse to let it go, then it still controls us and determines our actions. That makes us cling to ways that separate our spirit from our physical being, whether that be through hate or through egos or pride or whatever. I think that knowledge has stopped coming to us because we are not willing to release those things. Until we are able to release these things we carry inside of us, we are not going to be able to grow.

When AIM was growing spiritually as a movement, it had credibility with the people. Because AIM has stopped its spiritual growth, it no longer has credibility among the people. We have to really look at that to understand where AIM is going and look at what we can do to bring that credibility back.

c: Do you think that the so-called AIM paper wars that are going on are an indication of this "stalled" spirituality?

b: I think they are a clear indication of that. To me these are diversionary tactics that we allow to happen. What's being diverted away is the truth of what is really happening to us as a people. I can see what we're going to pass on to future generations, and it's going to hurt us and lessen our chances to survive as a people because we're not passing on knowledge.

Some of us have quit drinking. Some of us have been able to quit using drugs. But that's only a small part of it. There are things that each and every one of us can do to strengthen our circle as human beings. We're not going to survive as a people unless we base that circle on respect for all life.

c: Do you think that this grand jury investigation into Anna Mae's murder is another diversion?

b: Very much so. All these things like this grand jury investigation and these paper wars and the general suspicion, it's all diversionary. It is beneficial to the corrupt values system that controls all of us. When we get involved in these things, we lose focus of the real issues, and to me the real issue we are struggling for is the liberation, not only of our people, but of all life, from a corrupt values system that is destroying our natural identity with this land.

c: Do you think that identifying the actual person(s) that killed Anna

Mae will be of consequence to the true liberation of the People from a legacy of hatred?

B: I don't think that it's the issue here. Certainly the truth is at issue, but to me, it's not the truth of who or what killed Anna Mae. The real issue is survival. Anna Mae gave her life for a reason. Our getting involved with each other fighting about who's telling the truth won't work. We should confront what really happened to Anna Mae, and what really happened to her is a corrupt values system that is the enemy to all natural life.

Our people use incidents like what happened to Anna Mae like some of our people use alcohol. They use it to hide behind. It's easier for us to accuse each other than to face our real enemy.

I went through learning a lot of hard things in jail in South Dakota. I was accused of murdering two FBI agents from the fire fight at Oglala. I remember when they found Anna Mae's body. Anna Mae and I had become real close. I remember sitting in that jail cell, and I wanted to do something for Anna Mae. I was so angry that I wanted to hurt somebody. After the anger came this really lonely feeling that comes from feeling helpless in the world. I loved Anna Mae so much, yet there was nothing I could do but bang my head against that steel wall. To me, that was one of the loneliest times of my life.

That's when my life began to change for me, because Anna Mae came and talked to me in my sleep. Up to that point I'd been thinking about trying to escape from jail. I wasn't willing to spend the rest of my life behind bars for something I did no wrong for, so I was going to do all these things to stop that from happening, even if it meant making them kill me.

She came and talked to me. I didn't feel sorry for her after that. There was something more she wanted from me than my pity. I didn't have that strength, that understanding within myself about how to give to her and all our people. That's when I truly began to understand about the sacredness of life in this world.

c: What did you learn from what happened at Oglala?

b: There's a lot of confusion that came out of what happened at that shoot-out at Oglala. When we learn from our experience, then we cannot say that this was a mistake or that was a mistake—if we can learn something from it and not let it happen again.

When I lived at Oglala I carried a rifle, and I was willing to use that rifle. Each and every one of us that was there at that time was of that same mind. We were willing to die for what we thought was the continuance of our people. When you are willing to give up life like that, there are consequences. That's not giving something to your people that will continue on.

The thing that came to me was that my willingness to die out of the hate was wrong for me. I hated those people, not because they were the enemy, but I hated them because I was confused and did not understand my relationship to them. The young men that came there that day to fight with us, they too, carried the same kind of confusion because they hated us. They were confused and victimized by the same corrupt values system that gave both sides the energy to fight with such deadly force. It taught me they weren't my true enemy.

There are those of us who feel compassion for those men who were killed at Oglala and for their families. For me to admit that today means I have responsibilities now to fulfill. One of the responsibilities is to respect those people as my relatives. I couldn't do that back in 1975. Those of us that survived those learning experiences, maybe we understand that better now. We learned to use our minds more and our mouths less.

I think we haven't progressed as far as we should have. We still carry unspiritual ways within ourselves that the corrupt values system can use against us and against each other. If we truly understood that and our growth was continuing, maybe there wouldn't be all this pettiness that goes into these paper wars and accusations. Our focus would be on something a lot more enduring for our people.

c: Would you like to comment on Leonard Peltier's situation?

b: I think what's happening with Leonard's case is a real clear example about spiritual growth being stopped and being separated from the people. When Oglala came down, we were like a family who had been living together for quite a few months. We trusted each other, and we knew what the person was going to do under any circumstances. When people went to jail and people got killed, our family was still strong, and we still believed in each other and supported each other. We represented the truth of each other and the truth of our family circle. We wanted to add to the greater circle of life where all life is represented.

Leonard became a prisoner of war. He is serving two life sentences for something that he didn't do. I know. I was there. We were all there that day. Leonard represents a lot of things to the indigenous people of this land, and all these things relate back to the truth. If we allow Leonard to represent anything other than the truth, then we become victimized by this corrupt values system that is keeping Leonard in jail today. That is the lesson that is there for us to learn. For whatever reason, Leonard doesn't seek advice or direction from any of the family that was with him that day when Oglala came down and people gave their lives for what we're struggling for.

Leonard is taking direction from other people now. He's a desperate man. So he's willing to listen to anybody who comes to him and says they can get him out. That's part of that corrupt values system. Because he's insecure and isolated, separated from the people, it's easy for him to give in to it. He listens to other people—people who are telling lies about him and about what really happened at Oglala.

Like this book of Peter Matthiessen's, *In the Spirit of Crazy Horse*. It talks about that me and Bob Robideau knew about this guy who was coming to the camp that day in a red pickup, and he was bringing dynamite to us, and that guy now claims he is Mr. X. Well, there is no Mr. X. There was no man coming to our camp that day bringing dynamite. Those are all lies created to keep Leonard in jail longer.

When this Mr. X thing first started happening, we had a meeting in California. There were people there who were at Oglala that day. It was brought up about creating this lie about Mr. X being there and killing those men to raise support for Leonard's liberation. The final agreement in that meeting was the Mr. X idea wouldn't be used because it was a lie. We decided that because everything we had done so far was always based on the truth, and it was the truth that had liberated us in our trial, that when the truth finally came out, it would liberate Leonard.

I came back from South Dakota that year from the Sun Dance and was told that the writer from the movie, Oliver Stone, had come to Portland. He was picked up by a member who was there at the shootout that day and was taken to a phone. He talked to the guy who was supposed to be Mr. X who had shot and killed those agents. Mr. X supposedly drove down there in that red pickup after the shooting was going on. His shooting was supposedly a reactionary thing that happened when this agent looked up. Like it was more or less an accident or something. That is all totally false.

We have always maintained those agents who were killed were caught in the crossfire. The truck was operated by a man in the area who heard the gunfire and was worried about the safety of a family whose house was inside the compound. He checked the house, found no one home, and went on his way.

It is totally false that I had knowledge of who that person was and knew that person was going to come into our camp that day. I lost a lot of respect for Peter Matthiessen as a writer and as a person I could trust because he didn't verify this, and it put me and my family in jeopardy. He never made any effort to contact me and ask me if this was true.

I'm not going to cause a scene over this because I can't divert my attention away from the real truth. Peter Matthiessen was victimized by that, too. Whatever made him do that separated him from seeking out the truth. That's the important thing to me. What I represent is what I have to be concerned with. I cannot allow myself to become distracted by other things that do not represent the truth.

It's sad what's happening to Leonard today. I don't doubt that Leonard could be a free man, but it has to start within him. He has to believe in himself first, instead of believing in all these lies and the people bringing these lies to him. He represents a lot to all our people. He represents the agreements between the United States government and the indigenous people of this land. And all the violations of the treaties between two sovereign nations. Like them being there that day [the U.S. government] and causing that fire fight and the aftermath of it on that reservation, terrorizing the people to get what they wanted, which was a conviction of Leonard.

They also wanted a conviction of me and Bob Robideau, and fortunately we got to have a fair jury. I never have believed that we had a fair trial, because the only kind of fair trial we could have gotten from the U.S. government was no trial at all. We weren't guilty of anything. Enough of the truth was allowed to be presented in that courtroom by a fair judge that the jury would not convict us.

Leonard wasn't given that recognition at his trial—he wasn't allowed to present any truth. The jury wasn't allowed to see or hear or feel the truth. And he's been separated from it now. He's not lost, though. There's a way of going to the knowledge, and there's a way of not going to it. Until he learns the difference, he's always going to be a prisoner of war, whether it be physically or within himself. Right now I think he's a prisoner all the way because he's allowed himself to become separated from his spiritual being and has become confused enough to believe the lies. He needs to get back the truth, the truth that Leonard represents to all of us. Maybe that's the lesson he's there to teach.

c: Would you summarize the effects of the corrupt values system that is the true enemy of the people.

b: It's the values system that does not respect all life. It teaches us to hate each other, and it confuses us and separates our spiritual and physical beings. It's the values system that forced our people onto reservations in the 1800s and drove the Pilgrims out of England and brought them into our homeland. It's the values system that separates us from the natural world.

c: In the time you spent in prison in Canada, you spoke about having to understand why you were really there. Why were you there?

b: I was facing two life terms for the alleged attempted murder of two Canadian policemen. I remember walking into that prison in Canada and hearing that cell door close. I began to question Grandfather's wisdom. By then I had fulfilled my commitment to become a Sun Dancer for our people. I was a pipe carrier, and things were supposed to be happening for me in my life in a good way. I began to feel sorry for myself. At some point, something happened inside me, and I was made to look at myself and question myself. I had to admit that there were things I was doing as a spiritual person that I shouldn't have been doing. I knew in my heart that I didn't have the strength to stop doing those things. So the spirits put me into a situation where I was taken away from all the distractions around me. After I got over the self-pity and the anger, I was able to look at myself and see some of my own weaknesses. Once I was able to do that, I was able to start changing and to form some strength for myself with honor and dignity.

One of the things that helped me to do that was the guards. They gave me very "special treatment" there in the prison. I was always close to the front in the same cell so they could keep a close watch on me. Some of these guards would come by, and I could feel and see the hate in their eyes. I looked at those guards, and I began to see myself hating them. I could see the loneliness in their eyes and the pain they had that was coming from the hatred. I was being controlled by my hate, and I had to admit that. I had to decide that I didn't want to be like that. The number one teaching among all tribal people is to respect all life. When we hate one another, we are not capable of having respect for all life. The hate destroys us from within, and it destroys our identity with one another.

c: Did you think that part of why you were there was to help the native prisoners get access to ceremonies?

b: One of the reasons that I was there was to learn that it wasn't me that was important in this world. What is important is that pipe and what it represents. I thought that "I" was going to help my people with that pipe. I had to learn that it wasn't me that was going to take that pipe where it was needed, it was that pipe that was going to take me where it was needed. All I could do was find the courage in prayer to hang on and stay with that pipe. It didn't need me. I needed it.

Native people were not allowed to pray in the jails there at that time. My belief was that the power of the pipe was greater than any power in this world, and that power would take care of me and my needs in this world. So I asked to pray with my pipe and the sage and cedar and prayer feathers and everything I had been taught. It was denied, so that started the whole process.

I remember the first time I was allowed to "officially" pray within the walls of that institution. They came to my cell and handcuffed and shackled me and marched me out to the Protestant minister's office. I was allowed to hold an abalone shell with some sage and cedar in it, and I prayed that way. That was the beginning. In the end we had a sweat lodge, and I had my pipe and could keep it inside my cell, and brothers were fasting inside the prisons. It brought a lot of brothers together up there.

When I went to court, I told my lawyers that I wanted them to make a request that my pipe bundle be allowed to sit on that defense table. I said that the pipe bundle represents to me what the Bible represents to the Catholics and the Protestants. I wanted that to be represented in the courtroom. They met with the judge in his chambers, and the judge denied to even hear that argument in court. He said this was not going to be a "political trial." He said he was not willing to do that because it would be setting some kind of precedent. When the lawyers told us, I said to them, "Well, when we go back in there, I want you to make that request one more time." The lawyers made that final request, and it was denied.

I told the lawyers that since the judge denied that, I asked them to resign from the case and leave us there, and we would not present a defense. Because to let that man, that court, that government, separate me from my identity, then I was no longer anything. I would be nothing, and I had been that enough in my life already. I knew more than anything else in my life I did not want to be that anymore. If I allowed that separation in that courtroom from my pipe bundle, then I would become that again. So, the lawyers walked out of the courtroom, and me and Gary Butler sat there and presented no defense for two charges of attempted murder. We were facing life sentences on each of them. But we were willing to take our identities with us and live the rest of our lives inside those walls. We would not allow that identity to be separated from us again.

They presented their case and told all these lies against us. The jury would not convict us of attempted murder, even with no defense. They wouldn't believe we had tried to kill those officers, because we didn't. They were trying to assassinate us, and we were defending ourselves.

In Oakalla [British Columbia], they took me to a special unit that used to be death row. There was nobody in any of the other five cells. They brought Gary [Butler] in and put him two cells away from me. Right after lunch a man came with a welding torch, and he took chains and this big monstrous padlock and welded those chains together on our doors. That's how we spent the next six months. It takes a lot of hate to do that to another human being. That's why that pipe was needed up there. Because our brothers and our sisters inside those jails were hating, too.

The Indian people came to us and said that Indian people don't ask for religious rights up there because when they do, they get beat down really bad. There was a group of brothers in Saskatchewan that had tried. What broke them up was that they were strip-searched and sent defenseless into the yard. A group of white prisoners were given baseball bats and turned loose on them while the guards stood and watched. After this beating, they took the Indian brothers and shipped them out to different prisons. That's the kinds of things these brothers told us would happen to us and that we probably wouldn't find too much support.

I started asking for the right to have my pipe. My request was denied. There was a brotherhood with all the Indian brothers in the joint. I asked these brothers to support our request for ceremonies. All the brothers agreed. We put in the request to have ceremonies and sweat lodges. We waited a year. Then they sent us a notice that told us how we could pray and when we could pray. It was so distorted that it no longer represented our indigenous way of life. Nobody agreed to accept it, and that's when the struggle inside there truly began.

What evolved was a fast to pray for our oppressors because they were not only doing this to us, they were doing it to themselves. When this fast started, some of the brothers came to me and said, "I support what you're doing and believe what you're doing is right, but I can't accept starving myself to death." I said, "Just pray for us. That's all that you can do is just pray for us."

Gary started fasting first. Then they separated us because we were organizing. He sent word out that he was going to start fasting and praying for these people who were denying us these ceremonies. He was into his second day by the time I got the note. So I started fasting, too. About six days went by when Stuart Stonechild, one of the brothers who had been at Saskatchewan, joined the fast. It finally ended up there were sixteen brothers inside that penitentiary who were fasting. Some of those brothers were the same ones who said there was no way that they would starve themselves.

c: How long was the fast?

b: I fasted thirty-four days that time. Before it was over, Gary ended up clear across Canada. They ended up taking people out of there to separate us.

c: When the end of the fast came, what was the resolution with the system?

b: Their attorney general for the country was asked on the floor of Parliament why Indian people were having to fast to death for religious freedom in the prison system in Canada. He was asked, "Don't you think that's kind of embarrassing the Canadian people?" He got asked this two times by different people in Parliament. He got on the phone to Kent Prison right away and wanted to know what in the hell was going on because it was putting him on the hot seat [*laughs*]. He wanted it resolved right away and said, "Whatever they're asking for, give it to them."

They came and told us. But we wouldn't negotiate with the prison officials because we didn't trust them. They brought in a professor of law from University of Simon Fraser to act as our arbitrator. He had been in to our meetings before, so we all knew him.

We wrote out that we wanted a sweat lodge regularly; we wanted elders and our spiritual advisers to come into the prisons to consult with us; we wanted our pipes and ceremonies and the right to fast. We asked that since I was the pipe carrier that I would be allowed to go into another prisoner's cell to set up his altar to fast because the only place we were allowed to fast was in our cell. When it all came back, they had given us everything we asked for because that's how bad they wanted it to end. Then we had to wait again for about a year before we actually had our first sweat. It took that long while they dragged through the paperwork.

They changed national policies in the federal prison system by recognizing native people's rights to their ceremonies.

c: When was the pipe finally allowed into the court room?

b: It was the second time we went into court in 1984. Our lawyers appealed the conviction for weapons possession. The appeals court overturned the conviction and then said they wanted to retry us again. The lawyers met with the judge in his chambers, and the judge said, "Look, I don't want controversy in this. I expect you people are going to want that pipe in the courtroom. If it shows up in there, then it shows up in there, and it's all right." He didn't want to mess with it that time. [*Laughs*]

We went back to court, but by that time we had served four years, the maximum sentence on weapons possession. They wanted to keep us there as long as they could because we were wanted back in the States on a bogus murder charge. The States needed more time to work on their case. The Canadian government was willing to retry us on the same charges on which we had already served a maximum sentence and in which the guilty verdict had been overturned in appeal. It didn't make any sense, legal or otherwise, except the Oregon officials wanted them to keep us for two more years. The judge told us he had decided in his mind that he was going to sentence us to sixteen months. When he heard what our lawyers presented, he changed his mind and sentenced us to one day. They had no choice but to send us back down to the States. The Oregon officials knew they had no case, and we were fully acquitted.

c: Earlier in your life, when you were in the Oregon prison system, had native prisoners gained any religious rights?

b: When I was in there none of that was allowed. But it was the farthest thing from my mind in those days. By the time I came back from Canada, they were allowed to have sweats and grow their hair long.

c: The Oregon Corrections Division is supposed to be working on a systemwide policy for religious rights. Have you been involved in that process?

b: One of the prisoners began calling me about some commission being formed to develop a policy about native religious rights in Oregon's corrections system. His concern was that native people were not being consulted about this. One of the concerns of the prisoners is that this not be given to the jurisdiction of the chaplaincy. The concern of the brothers seems to be that if their religious rights are going to be determined by non-native people who believe in a different way, a lot of things will really change for them. The native ceremonies at Oregon State Penitentiary have always been under the Activities Department. Things have gone good that way without major interference. It's up to the brothers to make things happen and not on anybody else. If it goes under the chaplaincy, it will be up to them to schedule and determine when ceremonies can happen. The brothers can foresee difficulties.

They began contacting different people in the community for support and asked to be represented at these committee meetings and the public hearings in the communities. I think there were two public meetings supposedly held in the communities. None of the native people in the community were notified through the regular channels of communication. A few people learned about it somehow and went and stated that these meetings should be rescheduled so more people could attend. That request was denied by the corrections people. Corrections was supposed to use information gathered in these meetings to make their final decision about this policy. So there really is no community involvement in making this decision.

c: Were you on that original committee?

b: There was a committee that had been thrown together. I think there was a prison chaplain or priest on there and a captain of the guards. The native people on the committee all worked within the system and were picked by the system. The reason I got a call was that the Lakota Club, which is the brotherhood inside the walls, had wanted me to be on this committee.

I told them to submit my name, and I would do what I could. I got a letter from Corrections that I was on this committee. They said they would notify me of meetings. The next letter that I got said that all these decisions had already been made. I had never been invited or notified to go to any of the meetings. Yet my name was listed as making these decisions. And I am not the only native person who was asked for input and then not told what was going on until after the fact.

c: Would you comment on the women prisoners' involvement in this whole process?

b: As far as I can tell, there has been very little, if any, input from the women. They have not sought the women's perspective. The women's prison already has the chaplaincy in charge of the women's ceremonies, and there have been some real problems because of it. If the chaplain forgets to put out a memo about the schedule, then there is not going to be a sweat lodge ceremony. My understanding is that this happens more often than it should. They only allow the women to sweat once a month. If the women were responsible for taking care of this themselves, it would happen, because the women want it to happen. They are not having a chance to tell what they need and their perspective as women.

c: Do you think this has to do with how the dominant system generally devalues women?

b: Yes, and I think it's a purposeful effort by the system to separate the men and the women. This values system does that.

Respect for the women and our relationship to that power that is represented by the women is very sacred to all male life. The values system that seeks to control all of us has to break down that kind of values system that respects women and the female power, and that teaches us our identity as males to the female power.

c: If it is determined by the policy that it [native ceremonies] will be overseen by the chaplains, do you think it will ever really work?

b: No, I don't think it will work if it is under their jurisdiction because their belief doesn't allow for any way other than their own way.

c: Would having a paid native coordinator to bring in Indian doctors and spiritual leaders and whoever else is needed work?

b: Yeah. It worked up in Canada. We had a person who was affiliated with a native organization on the outside. He would act as our liaison with the People.

Our people cannot afford to give up their right to pray. They need those ceremonies and this way of life. It shouldn't be denied because they are in prison. Because of where they are, they may need it even more.

c: You have talked about the Fourth World prophecies. How do you see us being affected in this time by these prophecies?

b: When I first started walking this path, the teachers told me the earth and the people are going to go through four stages of purification before there is peace and harmony again. They told me that the earth was in its third stage of purification and that the people are in their first stage of purification. When Mother Earth goes into her fourth stage of purification, a lot of us are going to perish physically because we're not in our fourth stage. There will be some who are in that fourth stage who will survive, and for them life will continue on.

When you walk on the path of knowledge, sometimes you're going to find we have to leave some of our people behind. Life is a continuous learning experience. One of the things that slows us down in our spiritual growth is when we have people that we care about who are falling down around us. We're trying to follow this path, yet there are many of our people who can't walk that path. Because we love them, we want them to walk with us. Sometimes in staying there with them we stop our responsibilities of spiritual growth.

My teachers told me there are going to be times in my life when I'm going to have to leave these people behind, if I'm to continue to fulfill my responsibilities in our circle of life to help strengthen the future for our people. Leave them behind, but don't forget them. Remember them in my prayers and help them that way.

c: You're involved with Oregon Native Youth Council [ONYC] in Oregon. What is that about?

b: Oregon Native Youth Council, as it implicates, is closely associated with our young people. To me, the main concern of Oregon Native Youth Council is to break this trend of hate that is being passed on generation after generation. The youth council's purpose is to wake up our people to what we are doing to our children.

Look at what's happening to our youth today. Our youth are forming gangs and killing each other. It's really sad what is happening today on the reservations and in the urban areas. I grew up and saw a lot of adults drink themselves to death, knowing they were dying and yet they kept drinking. That's what we're concerned about—not giving that kind of life to our children. Because if this keeps on going for another two or three generations, with our people giving up that spirit to live, then we will not survive as a people or a nation. That's our responsibility to our young people today, to show them there is another way to go.

ONYC isn't just for youth who are getting into trouble. We want to support and encourage the youth who are doing well because they are strengthening our circle. They need to know that we appreciate them and the good things they contribute.

Anybody who represents Oregon Native Youth Council or works with ONYC has to understand that they cannot add to the confusion that is being used to oppress our people spiritually and physically. We don't advocate the use of alcohol or drugs or violence within our circle because we don't want people in our circle contributing to the downfall of our people.

Our long-range goal is to overcome the hatred and confusion that separate all people. But first we need to work with our people, and we need a physical land base to work from. We want to set up a permanent encampment in Oregon where youth can have a safe place to find the balance between the two worlds with the ongoing assistance of elders and adults. It will be a healing place, not just for the youth, but for all native people. So people can learn to stay strong in their identity and not be dominated by the current values system.

C: A lot of the young people that are involved in this mentality of anger and violence as a way of feeling powerful see themselves as being "warriors." Would you talk about your perception of what being a warrior means?

B: In this world there's two powers that we know. There is the female power and the male power. Everything else evolves from those two powers. Female power is the power that gives life and brings life into this world, and the male power is the power to protect that life. Being a warrior to me is just one part of our responsibility as males in this world. It only represents one part of the complete male power that says that we respect and protect life.

I don't know if there is a word in any of our tribal languages that says "warrior," because the concept of a warrior to me is a person who's always willing to go to war. That's not one of our teachings. There are other ways of respecting and protecting life. The concept of warrior has been corrupted by that values system that comes from the teaching of fighting out of hate for an enemy rather than out of love for our people.

If we're going to look at ourselves as males, as men, as warriors, we have to look at the whole being. We don't give up our right to defend ourselves or our people. We have to recognize the difference between a real threat and a perceived threat. But we also have responsibilities to be fathers to our children, and those young ones have a lot to teach us, too. We have responsibilities to the female power and to our women to nourish and protect that power. We have responsibility as men, as males, to our elders and to our future generations. We have responsibilities to our ancestors. They have a sacred place in our circle. We have to take care of those places. To me that's being a warrior.

C: Would you talk about what the children and the youth have to teach us?

B: I'm fifty-two years old, and during my life I fathered children that I didn't even know. I remember my first daughter. She was eight years old before I even knew about her or ever met her. My whole life has been like that with my children. I have two daughters and four sons.

Except for my last two sons, I don't really know any of my other children. That's how confused and separated I was in my hate.

These two boys that I have with me now teach me a lot of things. The innocence of our children is the wisdom of our elders from past generations. If we have the ability and take the time to look within our children's eyes and see what is inside of these children, we can learn from that.

One day I looked over at my boy, Che, and he was just sitting there looking at me. There was no expression on his face. I thought at first that something was wrong with him. Then I started looking at his eyes, and I started seeing another world through his eyes. This feeling came over me that he saw things in me that I still cling to because I am not strong enough or wise enough or courageous enough to let go of them. I saw that as long as I carry that weakness and that confusion within me, I cannot truly represent the identity that was meant for me to represent in this world. It was like my ancestors were looking at me.

This other boy I have who's about sixteen months old now, he has the same innocence. All of our children carry that innocence for us, but we are always thinking that we are the ones who teach these children and that we own these children. We don't look at our children and respect them like we should. We have to start thinking about what it really means when we say our children are the future and make sure there is a future there for them.

BUFFY SAINTE-MARIE

Around 1941 on a reserve in Saskatchewan, a baby girl was born who was destined to become one of the premiere native musicians in the history of Canada and the United States. This baby girl was taken early from her homelands and adopted by a family in the northeastern United States. At age three she began playing her piano and making up songs to entertain herself. This was the beginning of a musical and artistic journey for Buffy Sainte-Marie that continues into the present and has resulted in a myriad of contributions that remains unequaled.

She has earned a degree in philosophy, teaching credentials, and a Ph.D. in fine arts from the University of Massachusetts. After completing college in the 1960s, she was en route to India when she decided to "stop off in New York City and try my hand at singing." She brought a unique voice, its resonant vibrato carrying words of indigenous struggle and truths that had been left untold by mainstream singers of the day.

Buffy Sainte-Marie's songwriting ability drew attention from performers in nearly every genre. From Elvis Presley, Donovan, Chet Atkins, Janis Joplin, and the Indigo Girls to the Boston Pops Orchestra, literally hundreds of artists performed and continue to perform her songs. "Up Where We Belong" from the film *An Officer and a Gentleman* won an Academy Award.

Her boundless creative energy and work in music, visual art, writing, and teaching, combined with her dedication to indigenous struggles, have taken her around the globe to places like Europe, Hong Kong, Australia, and Japan. She has created musical scores for films and television. In 1976 she joined the cast of *Sesame Street* for five and a half years and was the only consistent native face on children's television. In March of 1996 she was inducted into the Canadian music industry's

Juno Hall of Fame. When *Coincidence and Likely Stories* was released, Sainte-Marie was named Best International Artist in France and received the Grand Prix Charles de Gaulle award. She has been an ongoing innovator in using the computer for both visual art and digital music, and she still performs on the world's oldest known stringed instrument, a mouthbow.

Currently Sainte-Marie is dedicating the primary portion of her time to the formal implementation of the Cradleboard Teaching Project, which is committed to developing native curriculum that is accurate and relevant in both reservation and mainstream school systems.

As Buffy Sainte-Marie continues with her multifaceted love of creative expression, she also continues another tradition—remembering her relationship to her ancestors and to the Creator. This is her foundation, and from it there is much good yet to come.

E. K. CALDWELL: When you were growing up, did you get to spend time with other native people?

BUFFY SAINTE-MARIE: There was one family who lived in the town where I was living, and there was a Chippewa man who was wonderful to me. He was really the only person who gave me a sense of native reality.

C: When did you get to go home to Canada?

M: I visited when I was a child, and in my teens I used to go back and forth. My adopted mom was part Micmac, but it's not as though she was living in the community. I was the first person in that family to really reconnect and explore the deeper meaning of a whole additional culture.

C: Were there other native musicians around New York when you started there?

M: Not really in pop music. There were people who were Indian, but who didn't have active roles in their communities. There wasn't anyone really singing about native life or spending lots of time in native communities.

c: You have crossed more musical borders than any other native musician. Do you think it's important for native musicians to have that experience?

M: No. I think it's important for native musicians to do exactly what they are inspired to do. If that is stay home, then stay home. If it's to dabble around in country music, pop music, the classics, movie scoring, grass roots music, or whatever, then that is what you should do. The important thing is follow your inspiration, like the Creator tells us to do.

c: How has being involved in all those genres of music contributed to your growth as a musician and as a person?

M: It's fun. I'm still the same girl as when I was three years old. I'm having a wonderful time with the arts and with the talent the Creator gives us all. Most of us are so accustomed to thinking that we get our creativity in European schools that we are cut off from it. The truth is, when we are made in the image of the Creator, we are creative. We create our children, our music, our paintings, and our futures. Nobody makes a buck off this, so you don't hear too many people saying it. The true self-empowerment from the natural Creator and the fact that we are intimately related to the Creator every second of our lives have been co-opted out of much of the world's community.

c: Did you ever think that you would make a living as a musician?

M: [*Laughs*] Oh, no! When I went off to college I thought I might go into veterinary science, but I discovered philosophy along the way. It became my first major. Then I got a teacher's degree so I would have a way to make a living. The combination of philosophy and teaching has been perfect for my own sense of communication in learning from other people and passing on what I have learned. In the native community there are so many people who are "under-recognized" but who are very powerful teachers.

c: Considering your background in formal education, do you think it's important that our young people get that kind of education?

M: I think it's not only important, I think it's fun. And fun is important. I'm interested in self-empowerment of communities and the individuals inside communities, and families and the individuals within the family. I think that it's just not said often enough that self-empowerment comes from *enjoying* what you do. A lot of people lay this heavy trip on high school students about, "You've *got* to get an education," and nobody tells them how much fun it can be to get out of town, go to a university, and choose what you're going to study. It can all be so amazing. But no, I never use the words, "You must" or "You should go to college." I just say that it's fun, a real gas.

C: Considering the slant that most of academia has on indigenous people, how can students avoid becoming propagandized by information they are learning in school?

M: There is a lot of work to be done, and that question is central to why I am not out on the road at the moment. The Cradleboard Teaching Project began as an idea years ago and addresses the question that you just asked. It is a great project, and the Kellogg Foundation has just given me a whole lot of money to continue it. That is why I have pulled back from touring.

I find, as a teacher going into mainstream classes, that even excellent teachers are at a loss in teaching an accurate and enriching Native American study unit when that "embarrassing time of year" comes around again with all the paper feathers and pilgrim hats. Sandwiched in-between Columbus Day and Thanksgiving are "where the Indians are," and most teachers all over the world complain there are not enough materials.

The other side of this is what really affects us. Native people of all ages suffer all our lives from being misperceived. We have mental health problems and self-esteem problems and feel disempowered, because are we *Dances with Wolves* or *Pocahontas*, or what are we? So, any of us who are in the fortunate position of traveling to hundreds of reserves, and indigenous communities that are outside of North America as well, can have an overview of richness and great contributions and incredible potential in the Indian community.

The Cradleboard Teaching Project puts Indian people in the

driver's seat of designing and delivering native curriculum and native identity into mainstream and other native schools. My attention is going to be devoted to this project right now.

c: When will the project be instituted?

m: It's actually already been going informally for almost twelve years, making connections between mainstream and indigenous reserve schools. They have all been in Canada with the exception of one interaction between Hawaii and Saskatchewan. The five sites are Lakota [South Dakota], Mohawk [New York], Cree [Montana], Northwest Coast [Puyallup, Washington], and Ojibwe [Minnesota]. There are only five pilot sites, and this year is just set-up time. If it works as well as the informal sites have worked, I have a feeling the question you asked will have a whole new answer. I feel that kids who are interested in self-identity, self-esteem, self-empowerment, which is just about everybody, will not only be able to learn but will be able to teach while they learn.

c: You have used the computer for both music and artwork for quite some time. What generated your interest in this technology?

m: It really came out of my curiosity and interest in sound. I've always been interested in sound and tuning my guitar in all kinds of strange ways because I have an unusual voice. I developed an interest in electronic music in the 60s, [*laughs*] and believe me, folk singers at that time had no interest in that. I made an album in the 60s which was the first ever electronic quadraphonic vocal album [*Illuminations*]. After that there wasn't really anywhere to go with it because it was too new. There always has been an audience for electronic music, but not the folk singer side of things, so I crossed over to the other side of the street real early. I like to do lots of things because that is what makes me happy. I liked electronic music, and about the only place that I could go to do that was in music scoring. In the 70s and 80s I went into scoring movies and did lots of them for film and TV, from big ones to little ones. During that time I switched over from electronic music made on synthesizers to the first music computers. The first one was a Fairlight, and the second was a Synclavier. In 1984 the Macintosh came out, and I found that I could do my music, my paintings, and my writing all in one machine! When I was done I could take a floppy disk on the road. That was absolutely incredible for me. I could take it right to the reserve or anywhere. I ended up making a record in a tipi out on the Plains in Saskatchewan just because it was so easy. That's how my interests evolved.

I'm not the only native person who was real early in computer technology. People thought I was out of my mind, even as recently as two years ago, for talking about Indian people and computers. White people were laughing up their sleeves, thinking, "That's a funny idea." That was really insulting. I said, "Okay, that does it. I'm writing an article"; so I did. It's called "Cyberskins" and is on my website <www.aloha.net/bsm>.

C: In terms of our involvement in computers and these newly accessible technologies, do you think it's important?

M: I think it's another option for us, and it's great. It's very ergonomic and very efficient. Like any other new toy, you might run up a big phone bill at first, but you learn to be more selective.

C: A lot of people are almost phobic about computer technology or, at the very least, intimidated by its function and implications. How do we overcome that?

M: Anytime that type of question comes up, I ask myself what the real point is to this technology. What I've come up with is: Number one, reality is your friend. Number two is that nothing will take the place of the fire. Just like a guitar does not replace the human voice. It is just another way to communicate music. Nothing will take the place of face-to-face interaction. A computer is just another way to communicate. It is a glorified telephone, piece of paper, typewriter. That's all it is. All it does is record and communicate your thoughts. It's not essential, and if people would rather not be involved, then don't be involved. It's nothing to lose sleep over. The real problem is not with the people who are resistant to technology. It comes from people who get a little head start over others and then say they are better than other people because of it. Anyone who is in the fore-front of technology knows better than to do that. There is always going to be somebody ahead of you and somebody behind you, and it doesn't matter. The bottom line is when anything is based on that old pecking order that Europe is constructed upon. Well, it has leaked into our Indian communities, and it really has no place there. Communication is good, no matter what you use to do it, and if you want to use a crayon today instead of a pencil, then go for it.

c: Considering the longevity of your career, and all the artistic borders you have crossed, did you ever feel like you were expected to repre-sent all Indian people all the time? How did you learn to deal with all that attention?

m: Mostly by luck, good and bad. For instance, bad luck for my career has generally been good luck for my heart and my spirit. I've never had a huge career like say, Madonna, or someone like that. I've al-ways had an underground career. It has been partly my own doing, because for most people what you are "supposed" to do for your ca-reer is to live in New York or LA and schmooze and socialize and hang with business and record and movie people. I have never really en-joyed that. My motivation has always been more to get to the closest reservation. It's kept me sane, [*laughs*] well, as sane as I get, about a lot of things. I guess the answer for me was to "go home." Anytime I started feeling like somebody's token Indian, I'd go to some reserva-tion and basically laugh it off. Obviously nobody in the Indian com-munity thinks I represent all Indians!

c: You have had good fortune with having your work in the main-stream. Do you think it is important for native artists, musicians, writers, to have their work out in the mainstream?

m: Well, guess it depends on what you want. A lot of my work I don't want in the mainstream. I have had many occasions and oppor-tunities to take my clothes off in Hollywood and be the Indian of the Week, but certain things appeal to you and others don't. The great body of my work has never been seen, and in many cases I don't feel I have matured enough myself, and usually I am right about that. I only want to put out quality work. I worked on "Bury My Heart at Wounded Knee" for years because I knew that I wanted to say something that was very important to me and to other people and wanted it to be just right. I wanted it to be rock 'n' roll, and I wanted it to hold your attention, and I wanted the music to be very simple. The words and ideas are giving you only one chance to charm an audience into listening to that kind of material, because they don't want to hear it. They skip over that part of the newspaper, that kind of book. They are not around people who are in a position to tell them about what happened to the American Indian Movement or what the gold and uranium rush have in common when it comes to the impoverishment of native people. And the intimidation and brutality that is involved in the attack on Indian people. Most audiences think you're crazy.

Like *Coincidences and Likely Stories*, which had "Wounded Knee" on it—well, it didn't get U.S. distribution. It was a lot for America to take.

C: You were part of the *Sesame Street* cast for a long time. What was the greatest reward in that project?

M: Just the feeling that I was succeeding in my reason for joining the cast. I had one reason, and that was to let little kids and their caretakers know that Indians exist and that we are not all dead and stuffed in museums.

C: What impact do you think TV has on our children?

M: Oh, television and video games. I mean, I like them, too, just like we all do, but what worries me most about them is the way it paves the way for addiction. You get a deliberate and planned adrenalin rush every twenty-one seconds with the average children's TV show. It sets your mind and your body up for an almost constant adrenaline rush, and you're going to grow up and try to get that somehow. Without it, you end up feeling empty, like something is missing, so most people seek that outside themselves. It might be drugs or sex or gambling or work, or anything. That scares me. I don't really have an answer for this, except we have to become more active in quality programming.

c: Do you ever think about being involved in that?

m: No. At this stage of life, I would not be the right person for that. I gave my all with *Sesame Street* for five and a half years, doing two shows a day and raising an infant. I know how hard it is, and until I had time to do that properly, I wouldn't even mess with it.

c: Do you think TV depletes children's creativity?

m: I don't think it has to, depending on what kind of TV it is. People who are in American business today are interested in addicting us to their product, period. They don't tell us this. I have never seen it in the newspapers. That's the name of the game when it comes to business today—addict the customer to the product. I think that we have to do everything that we can do to give children additional options, whether it's spending time with them at home, or getting them out of the house and doing activities, riding horses, making gardens, whatever. It is to the advantage of businessmen that they keep us on the couch. Although TV can be fun, we have to teach kids alternatives and additional options. Our various native cultural practices are additional options for our children.

c: There are more young native musicians, artists, and writers getting attention in the mainstream than ever before. What kind of counsel would you give to them about dealing with the pressure of being in the spotlight?

m: Go home regularly. Don't drink. Leave drugs alone. Get enough sleep. Respect yourself. What you are carrying is something very precious and very rare. Every time you step on a stage, or on an airplane, or every time you go out to do your thing, you are able to make an incredible contribution to the rest of the world. I'm not talking about the old ambassador thing. It's not like that. But you have an opportunity to make an incredible contribution that can last your whole life long if you take care of yourself.